MORE

WARDSHIP COUNCIL - MEANING
OST SUSTAINABLE SOURCES

SHEA
STO
SC

THI
SOU
EAS

MARK
PLAC

FUERT
HOTA HOTA
EL ENMASCARADO DE PLATA
KATERINA HERRERO
JUAN EDWARDO JARVIS
ANDRÉS PEDRO LEON
ROLANDO CONCEIDER
y FILIPE EMPRESA

SCOURED SEVEN SEAS
FISHERMEN WHO
CATCH TASTIEST FISH
SUSTAINABLE METHODS.
WILL ALWAYS PLENTY

O ÚLTIMO

E DECISION

ARE"

MIND
BLOWINGLY
TASTY

"SELFISH"

wahaca

THOMASINA MIERS

Wahaca Mexican food at home

HODDER &
STOUGHTON

First published in Great Britain in 2012 by Hodder & Stoughton
An Hachette UK company

1

Text Copyright © Thomasina Miers 2012
Food Photography Copyright © Malou Burger
Except pages 56, 73, 97, 111, 220 (left), 234 © Tara Fisher

A CIP catalogue record for this title is available from the British Library

Hardback ISBN 978 1 444 7 22390
Ebook ISBN 978 1 444 7 56920

Designed by BuroCreative

Typeset in ITC Lubalin Graph BT

Printed and bound in China by C&C Offset Printing Co. Ltd.

Hodder & Stoughton policy is to use papers that are natural, renewable and
recyclable products and made from wood grown in sustainable forests.
The logging and manufacturing processes are expected to conform to the
environmental regulations of the country of origin.

Hodder & Stoughton Ltd
338 Euston Road
London NW1 3BH

www.hodder.co.uk

Thomasina Miers first arrived in Mexico aged 18, and the country and its food had such an impact that she went back to live there. She opened up a cocktail bar in Mexico City and used her free time to travel the country and cook with some of Mexico's top chefs. After returning to London and winning BBC2's *MasterChef* in 2005, Thomasina worked for six months with Skye Gyngell at Petersham Nurseries in Richmond.

Thomasina and Mark Selby soon opened their first Mexican street food cantina, Wahaca, which promptly won the *Observer Food Monthly*'s 'best cheap eats' award. Wahaca has since been included in the Cool Brands list, and was voted London's best Mexican. Wahaca has now has sites across the south-east of Britain, including Covent Garden, Soho, Bluewater, Canary Wharf, White City and Stratford.

Thomasina is the co-editor of *Soup Kitchen* and the author of *Cook*, *Wild Gourmets* and *Mexican Food Made Simple*. She lives in London with her husband and daughter.

To all Wahacos, past and present,
for making Wahaca such a
stonkingly good place to work.

Contents

MOUTH-WATERING

WORLD'S BIGGEST PORK SCRATCHING?

TORTA-LLY DELICIOUS

MEXICO CITY 23 miles

WILD HERBS

OAXACA

From Mexico...

MEXICO

I went to Mexico aged eighteen and fell for the country and its food with all the fervour of a first love. Everything dazzled me. The place was alive and pulsing with energy and the cuisine was a world away from what I had expected; until then, I thought that TexMex was Mexican food and that all tequila tasted cheap and nasty.

What I discovered was a world of incredible colour and flavour: 200 types of chilli, hundreds of varieties of corn, strange fruit, and wild herbs and greens whose names I couldn't even pronounce. I learnt that Mexico was the birthplace of many familiar ingredients: avocados, beans, heirloom tomatoes, pumpkins, courgettes, chocolate and even vanilla pods, which grow in the rainforests of Veracruz. I found it all impossibly romantic. Here was a cuisine as regional as Indian, as diverse as Chinese and as fresh as Italian. Here was a country whose people were obsessed by good food and good eating, no matter how rich or poor. I returned home and waited for the penny to drop – waited for someone to open the first real Mexican restaurant.

Nine years on, there was a Mexican food stall in Portobello cooking incredible, authentic food, and a couple of bars serving decent tequila. That was it. Before my memories could fade altogether, I went back to Mexico and got a job opening and running a cocktail bar in Mexico City, determined to discover what the country (and its gastronomy) was all about. I used my free time to travel around. I learnt how the Mexicans employ a simple toolbox of ingredients, plus spices and herbs such as cloves, cinnamon, coriander and oregano, to create layers of flavour. I set about unravelling the secrets to the great, complex moles (sauces) and slow-cooked meats. I found exciting variations in regional dishes, and incredible ingredients indigenous to specific states. Almost a year later, I returned home determined to do something with that knowledge.

The trouble was, I had plenty of enthusiasm but no money. But then I entered *MasterChef* (and won it!), got a job at Petersham Nurseries restaurant and, shortly thereafter, met Mark Selby through a mutual friend (thanks, Georgie Cleeve!). Things were looking up. Fiercely bright and bursting with energy, Mark had spent his time since university working in banks, where, through his contact with restaurateurs, entrepreneurs and

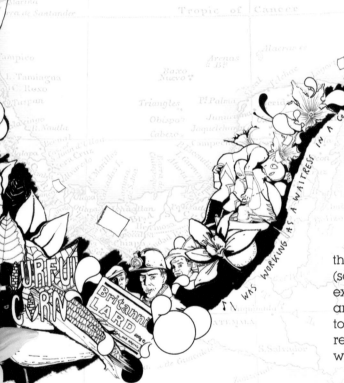

businessmen, he had learnt what governs the success and failure of small businesses. Mark is creative, meticulous and passionate. But the really amazing thing was that he was as crazy about Mexico as me. He had spent some time travelling around the country and, like me, he loved the food; also like me, he wanted to start up a restaurant.

We went back to Mexico together to explore our options, to look at cantinas, stalls and markets and to revisit the food. We had never eaten so much in our lives! In that ten-day trip we ate several breakfasts each morning, followed by a couple of

We knew that we were onto something. If we were this blown away by the incredible food, surely the rest of Britain would be too?

We considered the challenge. Some ingredients would be impossible to find back home. And selecting a menu would be tricky – there were so many styles of cooking to choose from, let alone recipes. We worked out that, although our menu

AND THE WINNER OF MASTERCHEF 2005 IS...

markets
street food
funky

...to London

lunches and then, occasionally, dinner on top. So anxious were we to try all the places on our list that we did not let up for a minute. With the generous hospitality that is a given in Mexico, everywhere we went food was lavished on us by chefs and restaurateurs. At night we collapsed into sweaty, dizzy heaps, plagued by our full tummies and overwhelmed by the different dishes, places and people we had seen.

would come from recipes found all over Mexico, what really inspired us was the food markets we first discovered in Oaxaca (Wa-ha-ca) and the way the stallholders worked together as a team to make the marketplace work. And we loved the spontaneity with which fresh ingredients were transformed into incredible-tasting street food right before our eyes. We loved the nation's approach to eating, which was

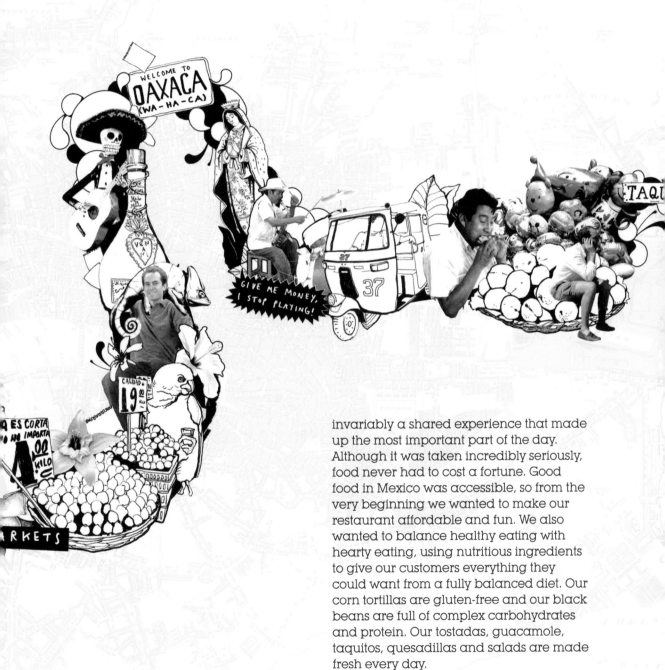

WELCOME TO OAXACA (WA-HA-CA)

GIVE ME MONEY, I STOP PLAYING!

37

TAQU

CALIDAD 19

ES CORTA NO IMPORTA 00 KILO

RKETS

invariably a shared experience that made up the most important part of the day. Although it was taken incredibly seriously, food never had to cost a fortune. Good food in Mexico was accessible, so from the very beginning we wanted to make our restaurant affordable and fun. We also wanted to balance healthy eating with hearty eating, using nutritious ingredients to give our customers everything they could want from a fully balanced diet. Our corn tortillas are gluten-free and our black beans are full of complex carbohydrates and protein. Our tostadas, guacamole, taquitos, quesadillas and salads are made fresh every day.

It took us a year to find our first site (in Covent Garden), a year to get the menu to where we really wanted it, and well over six months to come up with our name. We interviewed architects and designers, giving them a brief that matched our vision. We had to create something modern, fresh and totally different so that people would understand what we were about and that we were doing something

different from places that served just 'beans, beans and more beans'.

We were so nervous about the opening and our collective inexperience (the average age of our team in those early days was about twenty-five; I was the veteran at the ripe old age of thirty-one) that we opened by stealth and in the first week managed to feed a few hundred people in passing trade. In the second week, a few hundred more came, but the numbers were still low for a 140-seater

restaurant, so we closed off a large section to allow us to get to grips with the new business. A visit from a food journalist in week three frightened the life out of us, but he came, wrote a review and the moment it went live, our restaurant took off, along with a queue to get in that hasn't properly gone away in the last five years.

In that first month, such were our insanely long hours that Mark and I lost each a stone in weight, and we joked about hanging hammocks upstairs to save us

the commute to and from work. We went from ordering two boxes of avocados a day to fifteen boxes. Recipes that had been created in my kitchen went from feeding four to feeding 400. Five years on we have more restaurants and more staff, but we try to keep a sense of family at work. We have mad staff parties, highly competitive go-carting, occasional cook-offs in our homes and staff trips to our spiritual home, Mexico. We try to keep the prices low and the food exceptional. We like the idea that Wahaca is a place where anyone can enjoy a bit of the atmosphere and vibrancy of Mexican living.

Here are the recipes that inspire us and will, we hope, inspire you to share plates, roll up your sleeves and get stuck in. There are moreish nibbles, plenty of small plates of food for sharing, and some larger dishes that you can eat either with a fork or scooped into tortillas, with salsas and garnishes to taste. These filled tortillas are what street food is all about, and this is eating Mexican-style: fun, fantastic and full of flavour. Happy cooking! And when you're done, we hope you'll come to visit and tell us how you got on.

Tommi xxx

WHERE NEXT?

FROM MEXICO VIA LONDON TO YOUR KITCHEN ENJOY!

ESADILLA

a world of incredible dishes, and wonderful ingredients indigenous to specific states. Almost a

CORIANDER

BAY LEAVES

MEXICAN OREGANO

the Mexican store cupboard

At Wahaca we work hard to match the flavours of Mexico with ingredients that British farmers can produce on home soil. Since we believe in sustainability, we buy only British meat and MSC-certified fish whose stocks are not in huge decline. We use local ingredients wherever possible instead of flying food across the globe. Many of the cheeses available here have very similar flavour profiles to Mexican ones, so in place of queso fresco we use Lancashire, instead of panela we use feta, and rather than queso añejo we use Parmesan or pecorino. Herbs such as hoja santa, hierba de conejo and chepil would be wonderful to have, but aren't crucial when you can buy (or home-grow) good alternatives, such as tarragon, mint and oregano. In fact, you need only a relatively small selection of Mexican ingredients to make most of our recipes without fuss or effort. So stock up your cupboard and get cooking the Mexican way!

TOMATILLOS

Must haves:

Mexican oregano This comes dried and has a more pronounced floral flavour than standard oregano; a must for Mexican cooking and lasts at least six months.

Dried chillies Whether you are using anchos, chipotles, chile de árbol or guajillo, if you make sure you have a generous few handfuls of each in your cupboards, you will always be able to whip up a Mexican feast.

Pickled jalapeños Mexicans love their pickles, and a spoonful of these can be used to transform any number of dishes.

Tomatillos These are small, tart green tomatoes. If you search hard, you can get them fresh in the summer, otherwise you can order tins of them online for making the essential Salsa verde (page 242).

Spices No Mexican cook would be without cinnamon, cumin, allspice, cloves and black pepper for adding oomph to stocks and sauces.

Masa harina Made from finely ground maize, masa harina is the authentic flour you need to make corn tortillas (page 48): polenta and cornflour won't work. Buy it from larger supermarkets, healthfood shops or online (see Suppliers, page 242) and have a go at making your own. You'll probably want a tortilla press too; they're not expensive and will take out all the rolling work.

Onions, garlic, avocados, tomatoes, lime, fresh green chillies, bay leaves and coriander If you are going to cook Mexican, buy the lot and you won't be caught short.

Mexican shortcuts:

Stale tortillas can be transformed into deep-fried tortilla chips or delicious crispy strips to top soups and salads.

Chorizo By chorizo I mean the raw kind that needs to be cooked like a sausage – this is Mexican chorizo. Whenever I cook it, I save the fat in a little earthernware bowl. It keeps for months in the fridge and adds amazing flavour to frying onions.

Frozen tortillas I always have tortillas in my freezer to whip out for an impromptu dinner. The Cool Chile Company ones are particularly good.

Oil Try to keep a few litres of vegetable or sunflower oil in the cupboard for frying. You can strain and reuse it again and again.

Coriander makes a good substitute for dried epazote, a herb that has been used for thousands of years in Mexican cooking. Use just the roots and stalks, which have a much better, softer flavour than the leaves. I like to chop them finely and add them to the base of soups and sauces.

Frozen chillies Chillies freeze really well. I buy fresh Scotch bonnets, jalapeños or Thai green chillies and pulse them in a blender before freezing them in a small plastic container for future use.

Vanilla If you have some pods lying around store them in alcohol to make your own essence (see page 147).

VANILLA

SPICES

17

Chilli knowedge

RICH FLAVOUR

SALSAS MOLES MARINADES

Poblano (fresh) / Ancho (dried)
When fresh, the poblano looks like a dark green pepper; when dried, it is transformed into a round, dark red chilli with fruity tones. Rich in flavour and mild in heat, it adds sweetness and depth to marinades, salsas and moles. If you can't find ancho chillies, use Spanish dried red peppers instead.

Jalapeño (hah-luh-peyn-yoh)
Green, curvy, fresh and spicy, these fiery chillies can pack quite a punch, although the heat won't last long (and can vary hugely from one chilli to another). Substitute with any fresh green chilli, or add a few tiny bird's eye chillies for a proper tongue tingle.

FRESH

TONGUE TINGLE

PUNCH

UNDERTONES OF TOBACCO

LIKE THE ANCHO

Pasilla (pas-see-yah)
Dried like the ancho, but slightly hotter, with a herby, dried fruit flavour and undertones of tobacco.

LOOKS LIKE A CHINESE LANTERN

DEVILISHLY HOT!!

Habanero (hah-buh-nair-oh)

Habañeros are from the Yucatán, and are the first Mexican chilli to win Protected Denomination of Origin. They are almost identical in appearance and flavour to the Scotch bonnet and look like brightly coloured Chinese lanterns in orange, red and yellow. Pretty to look at but devilishly hot. Eat one whole at your peril!

Chipotle (chee-pot-lay)

This smoked jalapeño chilli is amongst Mexico's most loved varieties. It has an intoxicating fiery flavour that is delicious in salsas and mayonnaises, and makes the incredible Chipotles en adobo (page 238).

MEXICO'S MOST LOVED

DELICIOUS IN SALSAS

SLIGHLY SWEET CHILLI

FABULOUS WITH SEAFOOD

Guajillo (gwah-hee-yoh)

A brick red, mild, slightly sweet chilli that is fabulous with seafood. Can transform a simple dish, such as Fettuccine with chilli guajillo (page 109), into something spectacular.

Chile de árbol

Addictively fiery. The direct translation is 'tree chilli' because of the shape of the plant it grows on. We roast ours with garlic and mix with our Hot chilli nuts (page 195). If you can't get hold of the originals, use peperoncino, the small Italian dried chilli, as a substitute. or dried chilli flakes.

'TREE CHILLI'

FIERY

ROAST WITH GARLIC

BREAKFAST BURRITOS

Chocolate

bro

SET YOU UP FOR THE DAY

SUNSHI
FRUIT

THE HAPPY COUPLE ♡

eakfast

A Mexican breakfast is one of the greatest meals in the world. Among the finest I ever had was at a wedding in Oaxaca in 2010. As tradition dictates, the bride got up at 5 am for her procession through the village and was on her feet until midnight. To set her up for the day, sweet buns and Mexican hot chocolate were prepared for her and the whole village – a few hundred people – followed by turkey and the richest, darkest, most delectable mole poblano, all polished off by 9 am that same morning.

**M**ost days I am rushing about (so no time for banquets), but I can always fit in a Morning wake-up juice (page 26), a glass of flavour-popping goodness that is a cinch to prepare and packed full of vitamins. The 'sunshine' fruits in South America are on another level. Left on the trees and bushes long enough to ripen in the sun, they develop a sweeter, more pronounced flavour than we're used to in the UK, growing so soft and fragrant that they're completely irresistible. Back home, I search for fruit that is plump and fragrant, whizzing up the juiciest papaya, guava, mango, pineapple, apple and watermelon, maybe with some carrot, celery and cucumber (the combinations are endless), depending on whether I want a sweet start to the day or a super-healthy one.

If you're after a caffeine kick, a Real Mexican hot chocolate (page 25) is the most amazing way to wake up. Made well, with plenty of cacao, not much sugar and mixed with water rather than milk, it gives you a real hit, more rounded than a double espresso and not quite as strong. After our last staff trip to Mexico, we became so obsessed with the lighter, healthier hot chocolate they drink there that one of our chefs ordered a cacao-grinding machine and now makes the most amazing hot chocolate for all the restaurants.

To dip into your cacao, a sweet bun is irresistible. In Mexico City these are sugar-encrusted, anise-flavoured, baked with banana or clotted cream or layer upon layer of puff pastry and invariably followed by a refreshing plate of fruit, homemade granola and yoghurt.

Alternatively, Mexicans have a million ways to eat eggs: scrambled with chillies and sautéd onion, with cactus or ants' eggs; fried on leaves of hoja santa, or even with Oaxacan string cheese, on tortillas with slices of chorizo, with refried beans and always, always with at least a couple of freshly made salsas to dollop over. And, of course, there are baskets of steaming-hot corn tortillas to dip or fill or roll, and quesadillas stuffed with epazote, gooey cheese and some courgette flowers or mushrooms thrown in.

With such a spectacular choice on offer, it is tempting to make a day of breakfast, and some of the classic recipes in this chapter, such as Huevos a la Mexicana (page 37), will encourage you to do so. If it is a Sunday in Oaxaca, a leisurely brunch is most definitely the way to go (after all, it will be 3 or 4 pm before you have lunch). Take a trip to the market and you can expect a feast of sorts: grilled chorizo, skirt steak or strips of chilli-marinated pork. Plates of avocado or guacamole will arrive as accompaniments, along with tomatoes, radishes, chargrilled spring onions and wedges of lime, more salsas to anoint, more hot chocolate, more coffee. After so many hours of eating, and perhaps a cold beer to wash it all down, you may feel ready to go to bed again!

At Wahaca we sit down to a staff breakfast at 11 am to refuel and talk about the day ahead. Everyone has their trusty energy-boosters – the Avocado milkshakes and Molletes (pages 27 and 40) always go down a bomb. Here are our favourites to power you through the day or, if breakfast isn't your thing, to indulge in at any time of the day or night!

Real Mexican hot chocolate

Years before Hernando Cortés (1285–1547) brought chocolate to Europe, the Mixtecs concocted a cacao drink flavoured with spices and chillies and prepared with hot water. You can still get versions of this in Oaxaca today. Done well, with masses of ground, toasted cacao, the drink offers a healthy (yes, really!), rich, slightly addictive espresso-like hit; done badly, it is a watery, sugary mess. This version is my tried-and-tested way to wake up in the morning or at any time of day when I need a chocolate fix. Heavenly with warm, sweet rolls, such as the Pain de Miers (page 30).

Makes 4–6 espresso-sized cups
Time: 10 minutes

20 almonds, blanched
5mm cinnamon stick
1 tablespoon caster sugar
  (preferably vanilla sugar)
100g dark chocolate (at least
  70% cocoa solids), grated
  or finely chopped
450ml water

Heat a small frying pan and gently dry-roast the almonds and cinnamon until the almonds are lightly toasted all over. Put them both into a spice grinder with the sugar and grind to a fine powder. Add about a third of the chocolate and grind that too.

Break the remaining chocolate into a small pan, add the water and the almond-sugar paste and heat over a low flame to melt the chocolate. Beat with a whisk (a Teflon-coated one if you are using your best non-stick pan) to froth it up, or just stir to melt.

When the chocolate is just below simmering point, pour it into espresso cups through a fine sieve. It is rich, so you don't need a huge amount, but exceedingly good.

Morning wake-up juice

This juice is the most amazing bright green colour and so invigorating. It is a wonderful pick-me-up when you are tired, and a pretty good cure for hangovers too – the perfect antidote to one too many tequilas!

Put the celery, cucumber, apple and lemon juice into a blender and whiz until completely blended, then add the herbs and whiz again. If you have a juicer, just put everything through that. Drink at once.

Feeds 3
Time: 10 minutes

3 sticks of celery, de-stringed and roughly chopped
¼ cucumber, roughly chopped
4 sweet apples, peeled, cores removed and roughly chopped
juice of ½ a lemon
small handful of mint leaves
small handful of flat leaf parsley, roughly chopped

Papaya, carrot and lime juice

Ah, the taste of summer! The colours of papaya and carrot are lovely together and their sweet flavours combine beautifully. Get your juicer out: once you try something this wonderfully refreshing, it is hard to go back to anything else. A blissful way to start the day.

Put the first 4 ingredients into the blender and whiz. Add the apple juice or chopped apple, whiz again and taste. Depending on how sweet the fruit is, you might want to add a little honey or agave syrup. Drink at once.

Feeds 4
Time: 5–10 minutes

2 carrots, peeled and roughly chopped
1 papaya, peeled, de-seeded and roughly chopped
juice of 3 limes
juice of 2 oranges
200ml apple juice or 4 sweet apples, peeled, cores removed and roughly chopped
agave syrup or honey (optional)

Avocado milkshakes

Made with super-healthy agave syrup, these milkshakes are the tops: sweet, creamy and a stunning shade of green. The word 'avocado' derives from the Nahautl for 'testicle', as the ancient Aztecs considered this amazing fruit to be a fertility symbol. This became quite a joke in our kitchen, and Marcel, our barman at Covent Garden, started making these shakes for the guys every morning to power them through the day.

Feeds 3–4
Time: 5 minutes

3 avocados
650ml semi-skimmed milk
140ml agave syrup
juice of 2–3 limes

Halve and stone the avocados and scoop the flesh into a blender. Add the rest of the ingredients and blend until completely smooth. Drink at once!

Easy horchata

The classic horchata (or-chaa-tah) is a refreshing concoction of ground rice, almonds and cinnamon. It tastes like a milkshake, satisfying and cool, but is in fact dairy-free and amazingly nutritious. Whizzed up with a few oats and fruit, it will keep your batteries charged all day. This mixture keeps for a few days in the fridge, so make it in advance, enough to last for a few mornings. I love a lighter version without the oats or banana on blistering-hot afternoons when I am thirsty and my sweet tooth is taunting me.

Feeds 2
Time: 10 minutes

8 almonds, skins on
2 heaped tablespoons oats
ground cinnamon
1 medium banana
2 tablespoons yoghurt
   (optional)
300ml rice milk, almond milk or
   soya milk
1–2 tablespoons agave syrup or
   honey

Put the almonds and oats into a blender with a dusting of cinnamon (or more to taste) and whiz to make a fine powder. Add the banana, yoghurt and milk and blend until smooth. If you want it thinner, just add a little more rice milk.

To serve, pour into 2 glasses filled with ice and dust lightly with a little more cinnamon. This is also very good garnished with summer berries.

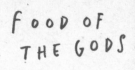

Oaxaca chocolate

BY GAVIN
KITCHEN WHIZ / CHEF TRAINER

I walked past a tiny, hot chocolate shop on the very edge of the main market in the centre of town. It looked old colonial – carved wood panelling, statuettes of mysterious gods, a small confessional box in the back of the shop, which turned out to be where you paid.

One side of the shop looked like a miniature factory, with sacks of cocoa beans, cinnamon sticks, toasted almonds and sugar. A man was standing underneath a small menu board that listed three recipes: basically different quantities of the four ingredients. I ordered version one and into the grinder next to him went scoops of the dry ingredients. Instantly, out came melted chocolate, like in a Harry Potter film, magical. Hot water was added and my Mexican hot chocolate was ready.

You know when sun shines on petrol spilt over water and you see the rainbow slick? Well, each bubble on the top of the drink had this and the taste was unbelievable. It was the same quantum leap as instant coffee to freshly ground espresso. Like tasting a rainbow. The cocoa butter with the actual chocolate – aromatic, sweet, bitter – blew me away.

A whole civilisation called, and still calls, chocolate the food of the gods, and now I know why. People with sensitive taste buds get hooked on this. Some claim to get a high on it. Good news, it is all true. I am a believer!

CACAO CRUDO
$60.00
KILO

chocolate

Banana, pecan and chocolate bread

The combination of bananas, sweet bready cake, melted dark chocolate chips and toasted nuts is a kind of nirvana for me, and particularly delicious first thing in the morning when I am feeling hungry. It requires the willpower of a Buddhist monk to resist wolfing the whole thing down when it first comes out of the oven, warm and enticing.

Preheat the oven to 180°C/350°F/gas 4. Butter and flour your loaf tin(s) and line the base with baking paper.

Mix the milk with the lemon juice and leave to one side (alternatively you can use buttermilk). Place the pecans on a baking sheet and lightly toast in the oven for 5–8 minutes. Set aside to cool.

Sift the flour, bicarbonate of soda, cinnamon and allspice into a bowl. Place the butter and half the sugar in another bowl and beat together until pale and fluffy. Gradually add the eggs with tablespoons of the flour mixture, then beat in the rest of the sugar, the bananas and the vanilla essence. Stir in the milk bit by bit. Roughly chop the pecans, then fold them and the chocolate into the mixture.

Pour into the loaf tin(s) and bake in the oven for about 50 minutes, until a metal skewer comes out clean. Leave to cool in the tin(s) for 10 minutes, then transfer to a cooling rack. This bread is delicious eaten slightly warm, but will keep for several days.

Feeds 6–8
Time: 1½ hours

125g butter, softened, plus extra
   for greasing
250g plain flour, plus extra for
   dusting 120ml semi-skimmed
   milk
1 teaspoon lemon juice
150g pecan nuts
1 teaspoon bicarbonate of soda
½ teaspoon ground cinnamon
few pinches of ground allspice
200g soft dark brown sugar
2 eggs, beaten
250g mashed ripe bananas
   (about 3 bananas)
few drops of vanilla essence
150g dark chocolate (at least
   70% cocoa solids), roughly
   chopped

NOTE: You will need 1 large loaf tin or 2 small ones.

Pain de Miers

In the markets in Mexico, you can wander through whole alleyways of shops selling sweet breads and pastries: doughy, flaky or crunchy, all ripe for dipping into steaming bowls of hot chocolate or sweet coffee. This recipe comes courtesy of a Twitter friend, @Doughblogs. Responding to my tweet for the perfect anise bun, he developed the 'Pain de Miers', which works a treat and which I have scarcely tweaked. Although the starter may look complicated, there is nothing to it, and it makes the buns beautifully soft and doughy. Baking these makes for the perfect contented afternoon and your house will smell heavenly.

First make the starter. Put the flour and water in a non-stick pan over a medium heat and beat with a wooden spoon or silicon whisk until it comes together and thickens to the consistency of glue (a few minutes). Don't let it colour. Using a spatula, scrape into a bowl, cover with clingfilm and cool to room temperature.

Meanwhile, put the milk in a small pan along with the golden syrup and the star anise and heat to dissolve the syrup and bring to simmering point. Just as the milk begins to bubble, turn off the heat and leave to infuse for 30 minutes.

Mix the flours and salt in a bowl and add the yeast, rubbing it in with your fingers. Transfer to an electric mixer fitted with a dough hook (if you have one), along with half the beaten egg and the starter. Slowly knead together, adding the milk mixture and, once that's incorporated, the butter. Turn up the speed to medium-fast and beat for 5 minutes. Keep an eye on the machine – it's working hard and may shuffle across the counter. Turn up the speed to full for a few more minutes until you have a completely smooth dough. If you don't have a dough hook, knead by hand for 10 minutes longer to achieve the same result. Put the dough into a clean bowl, cover with clingfilm and leave somewhere warm for about 90 minutes or until doubled in size...

Makes 10–12 buns
Time: 3 hours

150ml semi-skimmed milk
65ml golden syrup
1 star anise, ground into a
  powder
150g strong wholemeal bread
  flour
230g strong white bread flour
100g plain flour
½ teaspoon fine sea salt
12g fresh yeast
2 eggs, beaten
50g butter, softened

For the water-roux starter:
30g strong white bread flour
150ml water

For the glaze:
60g icing sugar
1 tablespoon hot water
juice of ½ an orange or
  ½ teaspoon vanilla essence
  (optional)

Once the dough is ready, divide into 10–12 fairly equal pieces, roll these into balls, then gently press down on each to create thickish discs roughly 3–4cm wide. The idea is not to flatten them totally, just make rounds. Place these on a lined baking sheet and score each one with 5 lines from centre to edge (see diagrams below). Cover with clingfilm, then leave to prove for another hour or until nearly doubled in size.

Preheat the oven to 200°C/390°F/gas 6. When the buns are ready, brush them with the remaining beaten egg and bake for 15–20 minutes, until they turn a lovely golden colour.

Make the sugar glaze by melting the icing sugar with 1–2 tablespoons of water over a low heat for a few minutes to make a paste. Whisk in a little orange juice (or vanilla essence if you like) until the glaze is thin enough to brush on the buns.

Take the buns from the oven, put them on a wire rack and allow them to cool for as long as you can bear it. Brush with the sugar glaze and enjoy, preferably dunked into mugs of Mexican hot chocolate (page 25).

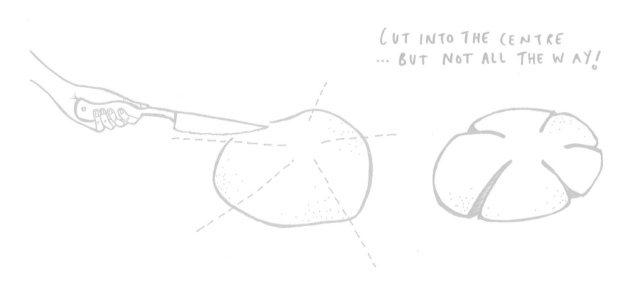

CUT INTO THE CENTRE
... BUT NOT ALL THE WAY!

Cakes' peanut cookies

I first made friends with the amazing Claire 'Cakes' Ptak (of Violet Cakes in east London) when she helped out on the styling for my first book, *Cook*. Arriving at the food shoot laden with homemade cookies, cakes and other irresistible treats, she was my kind of girl, instantly likeable and great fun. But I think it was her love of Mexican food that bonded us for good. At the time, I was spending a lot of energy persuading people that Mexican food was IT. I didn't need to try with Cakes – she was a devotee just like me. These cookies are adapted from one of her recipes. Mexicans love peanuts and cookies. We adore these with a strong coffee in the morning.

Makes about 25
Time: 30 minutes + 30 minutes chilling

180g plain flour
¾ teaspoon bicarbonate of soda
good pinch of salt
225g unsalted butter, softened
200g light brown sugar
1 egg plus 1 egg yolk
200g crunchy peanut butter
1 teaspoon vanilla essence
120g roasted, salted peanuts

Sift the flour and bicarbonate of soda into a bowl, then stir in the salt and set aside. In another bowl, or better still an electric mixer, cream the butter until it has turned from yellow to white and is light and fluffy. Beat in the sugar, then crack in the egg followed by the egg yolk. Gradually mix in the flour, peanut butter, vanilla essence and peanuts (reserving a handful to decorate the cookies with later). Place the mixture in the fridge to firm up for 30 minutes, or freeze until you want to use it.

Preheat the oven to 180°C/350°F/gas 4. Line 2 baking sheets with baking paper and drop heaped teaspoons of the chilled mixture onto them, spacing the blobs at least 5cm apart to allow them to spread during baking. Place a halved peanut on top of each blob. You will need to bake the cookies in 2 batches, so keep the second sheet refrigerated. Bake in the middle of the oven for 12–15 minutes, depending on whether you like your cookies crisp and gently browned or pale and squidgy in the middle, then transfer to a wire rack. Bake the second batch of cookies in the same way. Stash them in an airtight jar and remove when you want.

Corn pancakes with avocado cream and crispy bacon

I first encountered this breakfast at a boutique hotel in Baja California, where food influences go both ways across the border with the US. These corn pancakes are not authentic, but they are extremely good, especially with crispy bacon and cool avocado cream.

Preheat the oven to 160°C/320°F/gas 3. Cut the tomatoes in half and place them in roasting tin. Drizzle them with a little olive oil and season with salt, pepper and a small pinch of sugar. Roast in the oven for 30 minutes.

Meanwhile, if using fresh corn, stand each cob in a bowl, hold tight and use a long, sharp knife to shave off the kernels. Cook the corn (whether fresh or frozen) in salted, boiling water for 4–5 minutes, until tender, then drain. Finely chop half the coriander.

Sift the flour, baking powder and a pinch of sugar into a large mixing bowl. Make a well in the centre, break in the eggs and add a little of the milk. Start whisking and gradually add the rest of the milk to make a lump-free batter. Melt the butter and add half to the mixture, then fold in the corn, spring onions and chopped coriander. Taste and season with salt and pepper.

Heat a heavy-bottomed, non-stick frying pan until it is smoking hot, then brush with a little of the remaining melted butter. Dollop in 2 tablespoons of the corn mixture, spaced well apart so that the 2 pancakes don't run into each other (or make them one at a time if your pan is small). Fry over a medium heat for about 2 minutes a side until golden brown. Tansfer the cooked pancakes to a plate, cover with foil and keep warm in a low oven.

Whiz up the avocado cream ingredients in a blender until smooth and season to taste. Fry the bacon on a high heat with a drizzle of olive oil. Serve family and friends with a couple of pancakes, topped with 2 tomato halves, a sprinkling of coriander leaves, a generous dollop of the avocado cream and the crispy bacon. Eat at once!

Feeds 4–5
Time: 30 minutes

4–5 large, ripe plum tomatoes
1 tablespoon extra virgin
   olive oil
sea salt and freshly ground
   black pepper
few pinches of sugar
4 corn cobs or 450g frozen corn
large handful of coriander
180g plain flour
1 teaspoon baking powder
2 eggs and 2 egg yolks
140ml milk
40g butter
3 spring onions, finely sliced
8–10 rashers of streaky bacon

For the avocado cream:
2 avocados
juice of 1 lime
1 small garlic clove
2 tablespoons crème fraîche

Huevos Motuleños

This egg and tortilla breakfast comes from Motul, a tiny town in Puebla that has lent its name to a handful of famous Mexican dishes. Although this is in the breakfast section, it is easily substantial enough for lunch or a brilliantly satisfying supper. I can also report that it is perfect following late-night dancing in Mexico City. The original huevos Motuleños is served with peas; I like mine with spinach, some fried plantain and a hot sauce (which is what you'll find here). This is a good standard recipe, so perfect for getting creative with any other ingredients that take your fancy.

Whiz up the onion, garlic, cumin, cloves and thyme in a blender with a tablespoon of water. Heat 2 tablespoons of olive oil in a frying pan and, as soon as it's sizzling hot, add the onion mixture and stir, letting the raw onion flavour cook out for a few minutes. Add the chopped tomatoes and season well with salt and pepper.

Put a drizzle of oil in a fresh pan, add the spinach, season with salt, pepper and nutmeg and cook for a few minutes over a medium heat until the spinach has wilted. Add another 2 tablespoons of oil to the tortilla pan and, when it is hot, fry the eggs in batches of 2 over a high heat, so that the whites are nicely crisp on the outside and the yolks are still just runny. Peel and slice the plantain into 1 to 2cm discs and fry in the oil until golden brown on both sides, then drain on kitchen paper.

Meanwhile, warm your refried beans. In another frying pan, heat 2 tablespoons of oil and fry the tortillas (or pitas), on both sides until crisp, then put on 2 plates.

Put a tortilla on each plate, then spread with the warm refried beans and sprinkle with grated cheese (if I don't have any beans in the larder, hummus is a delicious if decidedly untraditional substitute). Top with 1 or 2 eggs, the Roast tomato salsa, spinach (or peas, if using), ham and plantain and tuck right in.

Feeds 2
Time: 20 minutes

½ onion, roughly chopped
2 garlic cloves
¼ teaspoon ground cumin
good pinch of ground cloves
sprig of thyme
olive oil, for frying
4 tomatoes, roughly cubed
sea salt and freshly ground black pepper
corn tortillas or pitta breads
200g spinach or 75g cooked peas, if you prefer
pinch of grated nutmeg
2–4 eggs (depending how hungry you are)

To serve:
3 tablespoons Refried beans (page 148) or hummus
Cheddar cheese, grated
Roast tomato salsa (page 233), or just some roast tomatoes (page 35), blitzed
2 slices good quality ham (optional)
1 ripe, almost black plantain, chopped (optional)

Huevos a la Mexicana

If you like your breakfasts big and easy, you'll love these Mexican scrambled eggs. Depending on how much chilli you favour, you can make them as mild or as spicy as you like, but I like to finish mine with some Roast tomato salsa (page 233) – our foolproof cure for the steamiest of hangovers!

Heat the fat in the pan until sizzling gently, then add the onion and chilli (de-seeded if you want your eggs less spicy). Cook for about 5 minutes over a medium to low heat so that the onion softens without colouring. Add the garlic and continue to cook on a low heat. Meanwhile, scoop the seeds from the tomatoes, dice the remaining flesh and add to the pan.

Whisk the eggs with the milk, season with salt and pepper, then pour into the onion mixture, stirring and gently heating through until they start to scramble. Cook as you like your eggs, runny or set, being wary that they carry on cooking after you have turned the heat off.

Sprinkle with the chopped coriander and serve with warm corn tortillas, your favourite hot salsa and a mug of strong coffee.

TIP: Save the tomato seeds for a soup or sauce.

Feeds 4
Time: 25 minutes

2–3 tablespoons melted lard or
    olive oil
1 white onion, finely chopped
1 fresh red chilli, finely chopped
2 garlic cloves, crushed or finely
    chopped
3 plum tomatoes, quartered
10 eggs
1 tablespoon milk
sea salt and freshly ground
    black pepper
large handful of coriander
    leaves, roughly chopped
warm corn tortillas, to serve

Rosie's breakfast burritos

Rosie, our organisational wizard at Wahaca, joined us in 2010 and is a massive fan of Mexico, having lived there in her early twenties. This is one of her favourite recipes and, as she says, 'The perfect breakfast or brunch after a night out on the mezcal' (see page 200 for more about that). Burritos are from northern Mexico and are brilliant for wrapping up any number of delicious ingredients in one great bundle.

Fry the bacon with a drizzle of olive oil in a non-stick pan over a high heat until crispy, then set aside somewhere warm. In the same pan, add another splash of oil, throw in the onion and cook on a low heat until soft but clear.

Meanwhile, beat the eggs lightly with a fork and add the milk (if using). Once the onions are soft, add the butter and, as it starts to melt, add the beaten eggs and a good grinding of salt and pepper and keep stirring on a low heat until they come to your preferred consistency. In Mexico they tend to like them very well done; I prefer them runny, so I take the pan off the heat just as they are starting to scramble, stirring all the while so they don't stick.

Spoon the scrambled eggs into the middle of each warm tortilla, add some avocado, then crumble in the crispy bacon and add the grated cheese. Roll up as shown opposite and, if you like, fry again for a few minutes a side to get a toasted crisp burrito. Deeeeelish!

Feeds 2
Time: 10 minutes

4 rashers of bacon
olive oil, for frying
½ small onion, finely diced
4 eggs
splash of milk (optional)
good knob of butter
sea salt and freshly ground
  black pepper
1 ripe Hass avocado, sliced
handful of grated Cheddar or
  any mature hard cheese
4 warm flour tortillas

PLACE FILLING IN
CENTRE OF TORTILLA...

FOLD OUTSIDE EDGES IN
AND SQUASH INGREDIENTS...

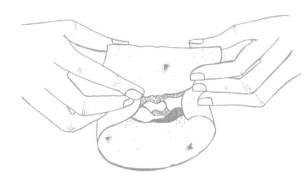

ROLL IT UP...

AND TUCK IN AT ONCE!

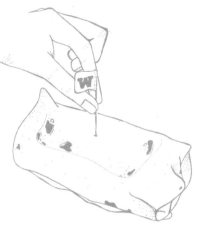

Molletes

Molletes are incredibly simple, satisfying sandwiches of
refried beans, melted cheese and fresh tomato salsa. In
Mexico they are eaten for breakfast or in the evening as
a light snack (after those legendarily long lunches). Don't
be fooled into thinking the ingredients look ordinary;
somehow this combination makes for the perfect fix.

Preheat the grill.

Cut the buns in half and toast the open sides under the grill
or in a dry frying pan or wide toaster. Butter both halves,
then spread the bottom halves with refried beans. Sprinkle
the grated Cheddar over the beans, then place under the
grill until the cheese starts to melt.

Garnish with the Fresh tomato salsa and, if you like, a
drizzle of crème fraîche. Pop on the lids and eat up at once!

Feeds 4
Time: 10 minutes

4 ciabbata buns
25g softened butter
**½ quantity Refried beans
(page 148)**
**100g extra mature Cheddar
cheese, grated**
**1 quantity Fresh tomato salsa
(page 232)**
50ml crème fraîche (optional)

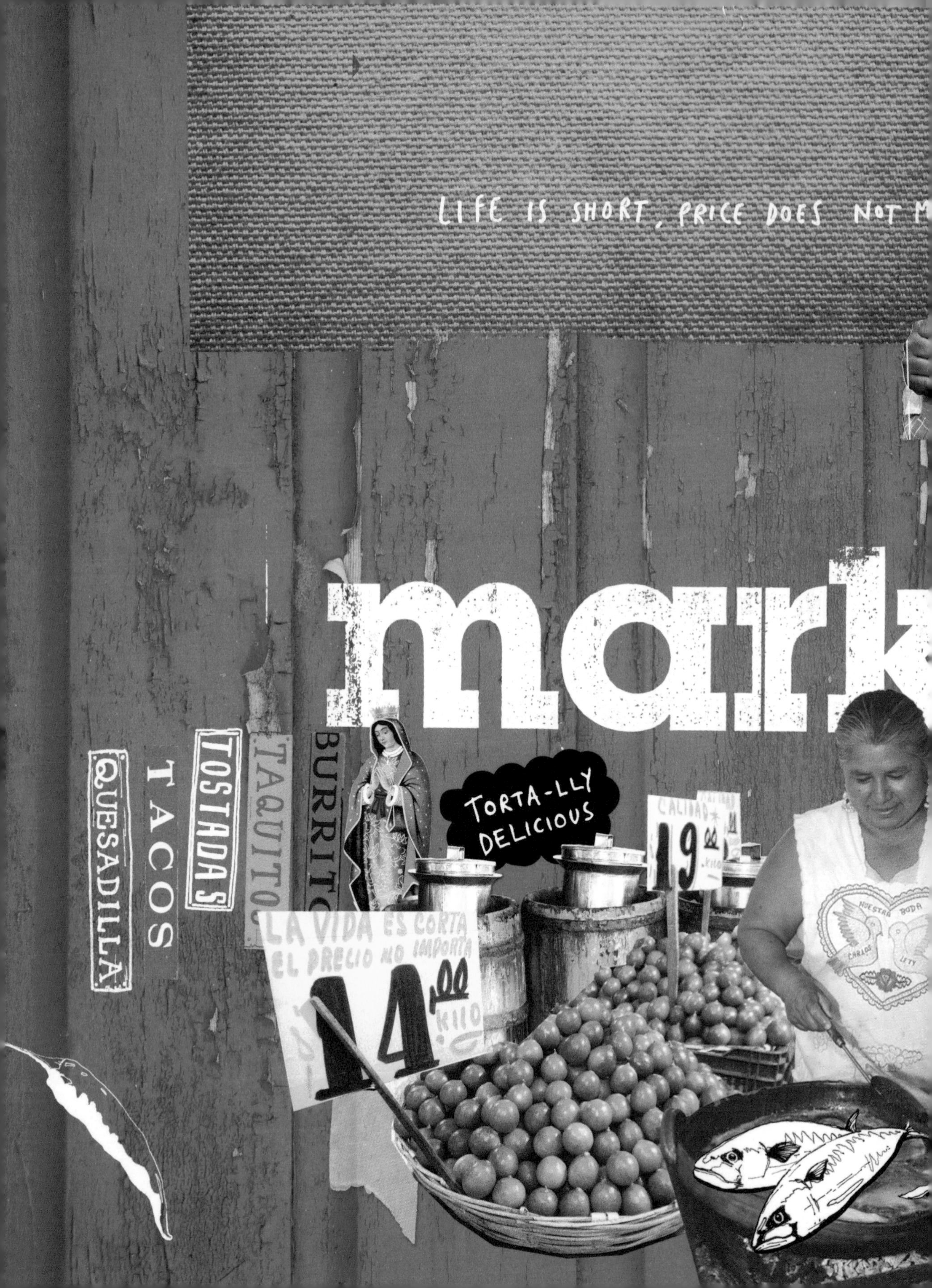
LIFE IS SHORT, PRICE DOES NOT
mark
QUESADILLA
TACOS
TOSTADAS
TAQUITO
BURRITO
TORTA-LLY DELICIOUS
LA VIDA ES CORTA
EL PRECIO NO IMPORTA
14.00 KILO
CALIDAD
19.00 KILO
NUESTRA BODA
CARLOS
LETY

SOLO ESTE DIA
$**6**$^{50} KILO

QUE NO FALTE EN SU MESA
$**3**$^{00} KILO

EMPANADAS

et food

A trip around the markets in Mexico is intoxicating. We speak a lot about the colour and freshness and rich culture of market eating to our team at Wahaca – throwing around words such as 'vibrant', 'colourful', 'friendly', 'fragrant', 'inspirational', 'exciting'... **Truly, words can hardly do the experience justice.**

CALIDAD
$**10**$^{00} KILO

**M**exico is one of the most bio-diverse countries in the world, and the beauty and abundance of what's on offer at the local markets is a joy. Everywhere you look, there are fresh fruits and vegetables in a kaleidoscope of colour, and towers of fresh and dried chillies: small, round, skinny, long, all with their own incredible flavour and character, and a different selection at each market, depending on which state you are in and what the local varieties are. Much on offer will have been picked that very morning and driven into the town or city for selling – Mexicans take great pride in using only the freshest of ingredients.

Markets are bustling, noisy places, always full of music and laughter. You visit them to shop, to meet friends and share a little gossip, and to eat. Wander around for long enough through the bread stands, the dairy section, the meat and the fish aisles and inevitably you will reach the spot frequented by locals, at any time of day, for their favourite tacos, tostadas and quesadillas.

Since lunch in Mexico is never before 2 o'clock at the earliest, the tummy rumble I used to get mid-morning (having breakfasted on a litre of fresh guava and papaya juice) was always my cue to find a tasty stopgap. But choosing what to order is hard! Should it be a tostada topped with sweet crabmeat and fruity, fiery habañero or chipotle-spiked prawns, a bowl of buttery sweet Esquites (page 53), or a mouth-watering empanada (page 71)?

Positioned in front of comals (open-fire cookers) are the taco stands. In Mexico, as you travel into the different regions, your tacos can come in glorious Technicolor: red, dark blue, inky black, yellow or white, according to the different hues of corn grown in the stallholder's fields. The mounds of wet corn dough come in hundreds of varieties. The fillings are stunningly good: wild greens spiked with fresh herbs and chillies; lightly truffled huitlacoche; courgette flowers with ricotta; long-braised meats, including cuts such as tongue, stomach and trotters, as well as seared steak with the smokiest sauce and naughty, melted cheese (page 60).

There are stalls offering barbacoa – goat, lamb or kid, slow-cooked overnight in large pit barbecues; great bubbling cauldrons of Pozole (page 134); seafood – and what a range of seafood! – freshly caught sea bass, ceviche, 'prawn coctel' (a scrummy mix, half seafood starter, half Virgin Mary); and a variety of seasonal delicacies stuffed inside empanadas or quesadillas. Grab a tortilla, point, gesture and smile, and the street vendor will delight in helping you to taste your way through his wares; Mexicans invariably take great pride in their cooking.

These corners of the market are an assault on the senses, with the shouts of the vendors, the flamboyant colours and the irresistible smells – sizzling meat, toasting corn, melting cheese, bubbling stews, limes and oranges and aromatic herbs – vying for your attention.

Eating elevenses or snacking at any time of day in Mexico can be something magnificent and splendid whatever your budget. At home, this street food will make an easy lunch, or mix and match a few recipes at the table to make a fun dinner with friends. Just get people to dive in and help themselves.

This food is at the heart of what we do at Wahaca and it is so easy to make at home. Experiment with the recipes and work out if you like a dish in a taco, on a tostada or grilled and put in tortas and quesadillas. Most of all, just have a ball.

Taco Famous, yet misunderstood, 'taco' to most Europeans means a crisp shell filled with chilli con carne. However, traditional tacos from Mexico are soft, freshly milled corn tortillas with delicious fillings (similar to a Chinese pancake). Salsas and hot sauces are added before the taco is half-rolled, half-folded and eaten.

Our taco recipes can be eaten as a starter or served with rice and/or beans for supper, allowing 4 or 5 small tacos per person or a couple of larger ones. The plan here is to eat like the Mexicans, so these are great served alongside other dishes for fun sharing, or have the fillings on bruschette, tostadas, quesadillas or burritos – this is your chance to get creative!

Quesadilla (kay-sah-dee-uh) comes from the Spanish, meaning 'little cheesy thing'. Tortillas are filled with ingredients such as spicy chicken, chorizo and potato, sautéd aubergine, mushroom and usually some kind of cheese, such as Oaxacan string cheese, which is gooey, like mozzarella. They are then folded and griddled until the inside is melting hot and the outside toasted.

It's a wrap

Taquito (tah-kee-toh) means 'little taco'. It consists of a small corn tortilla, filled with ground or shredded meat or fresh vegetables, rolled up into a narrow flute shape and lightly fried. Naughty but very nice.

Burrito From the northern state of Chihuahua, burritos are large flour tortillas, toasted hot and wrapped around a variety of freshly cooked ingredients. A meal in itself, a burrito provides the body with everything it needs for the day... and sometimes a little bit more! Hearty and satisfying.

Tostada A small tortilla gently fried or toasted until crisp (as on page 54) and topped with assorted fresh ingredients. It is lighter than a taco, and piled high with refreshing, beautifully prepared salady toppings. Tostadas are typically eaten as a snack or an accompaniment to something more substantial. Delicate but moreish.

Easy-peasy flour tortillas

When I was younger, I turned my nose up at flour tortillas. The wraps you found in British supermarkets were so uninspiring (they're getting better) and Mexico's corn tortillas had infinitely more depth of flavour. Then I tried my first proper flour tortilla in Baja California, enriched with delicious lard. I have never looked back. This is a very simple recipe for a papery thin tortilla, just like you find in market stalls across northern Mexico. I made these for a Mexican recently and she declared them the best flour tortillas she had ever tasted!

Put the flour in a large bowl and rub in the lard with your fingertips until it is fully incorporated. Add a teaspoon of salt, make a well in the middle of the flour and add half the water. Stir with a fork to incorporate the water, and keep adding the rest little by little until you pull the mixture together in a soft, pliable dough. This should not be sticky to touch. Once it has come together, knead for about 5 minutes on a floured board, then transfer to a clean bowl, cover with a damp cloth and leave to rest for 20 minutes.

When you are ready to make the tortillas, pick up the dough (it should be pretty smooth and elastic by now) and divide into balls about the size of a golf ball. Keep them covered with a damp cloth. Dust the board and your rolling pin with a little flour. Press a ball of dough firmly on the board with two fingers to flatten it into a fat pancake, then roll out to about 2mm thick. Place a frying pan over a medium-high heat and brush it with a smear of vegetable or olive oil.

Fry the tortillas on each side until they are puffed up and golden in patches. Wrap in a napkin, place in a bread basket and keep in a low oven (about 100°C/212°F/gas ¼) until you are ready to serve them.

Makes about 10 tortillas
Time: 40 minutes

250g strong white flour, preferably organic
4 heaped tablespoons lard or shortening, straight from the fridge
fine sea salt
approx. 500ml hand-hot water
oil, for frying

NOTE: You will need a rolling pin.

Perfect
corn tortillas

Using the soft corn tortilla (tor-tee-ya) as its base, street food originated from farmers' wives taking the midday meal out to the fields, using tortillas as the wrapping. Traders began offering this familiar 'home-cooked' food to newcomers to the city, and stalls sprang up selling regional favourites, giving rise to perhaps the most diverse cuisine of all the Americas. These wraps are the real McCoy: soft, supple, bursting with flavour and so much better than anything out of an air-sealed packet!

Put the flour in a large bowl and mix in the salt. Make a well in the centre and gradually add the hot water, stirring at first with a wooden spoon, then kneading with your hands until a dough forms. Add more water if necessary; you want the consistency of a soft clay, very lightly sticky. Gently knead for a couple more minutes, then cover with a damp tea towel and leave to rest for 20 minutes.

Make little balls from the dough, just bigger than a 50-pence piece, and cover them with a damp cloth. Place a frying pan over a medium-high heat and brush with a smear of vegetable or olive oil.

Put one half of the plastic bag on the tortilla press or a board and place a ball of dough in the middle. Using two fingers, gently squash it into a thickish disc. Cover with the other half of the bag and press or roll out until about about 3mm thick.

Peel away the top plastic, then flip the tortilla onto the palm of your hand. Peel off the plastic and turn the tortilla into the lightly oiled pan. Fry on one side for 20–30 seconds, until lovely browned spots appear underneath. If you're lucky, it may even puff up! Turn and cook for another 30 seconds, then turn once more.

Wrap in a tea towel and keep in a warm oven until you are ready to eat – there is nothing as unappetising as a cold tortilla.

Makes about 10 tortillas
Time: 35 minutes

250g masa harina flour
½ teaspoon fine sea salt
400ml hand-hot water
dash of oil

NOTE: You will need a plastic food bag cut into its 2 halves, and (preferably) a tortilla press, although you can just about get by with a rolling pin.

A little lard goes a long way...

The Mexicans believe in nose-to-tail-eating. Put more simply, they don't believe in wasting anything. Lard, being pig fat, is the by-product of cooking pork and, although many Mexican salsas don't use any fat at all, when it is used, lard is often the fat of choice. This is not just because it is so readily available but also because it tastes so good. It adds a depth of flavour that is impossible to reproduce when using sunflower oil or butter. Whilst many would be horrified by the notion of cooking with lard, as it has a reputation for being unhealthy, at Wahaca we think most things are good in moderation (save for additives and preservatives which we try to avoid). So go out and buy a pack of lard and stick it in the freezer where it will last for many months, or in the fridge where it will last for a few months.

Totopos

Totopos are tortilla chips to you and me, but in Mexico they are homemade, fried in oil until crisp and golden, which makes them altogether irresistible. They are so easy to make, and their flavour knocks the socks off bought chips, as you will discover should you proffer a bowl to friends before dinner with a salsa or two; they disappear in seconds! At home, this recipe is a great way to use up stale tortillas.

Heat the vegetable oil in a large casserole or saucepan until it is shimmering hot, leaving a good few inches at the top of the pan to allow the oil to bubble up.

Meanwhile, cut the tortillas into triangles or thin strips. I like to cut mine into fairly big triangles so that my friends can see that they are homemade and appreciate the effort! For an authentic garnish for soups and salads, cut the tortillas into small slivers, odd shapes or large shards, depending how you want your finished dish to look.

Test a sliver in the hot oil. If the oil bubbles up like mad, then it is up to temperature.

Deep-fry the tortillas until they turn a pale golden colour and crisp up. Remove with a slotted spoon and drain on plenty of kitchen paper before sprinkling with sea salt.

Cook the tortillas in batches so that you don't overcrowd the pan and bring the temperature of the oil down too much, as this can lead to soggy chips. Hot oil is essential for crisp, golden chips.

NOTE: You can make these with flour tortillas, although they will not have the same flavour as corn, and tend to absorb more oil. If you are using fresh corn tortillas leave them out for a few hours to dry out. They will fry much better and absorb less oil.

Time: 10 minutes

**vegetable oil, for deep-frying
  (at least 1 litre)
heap of corn tortillas
sea salt**

Market food

Chilli-spiked grilled corn

My rule is to make one of these per person and then a few more for luck – they seem to disappear as fast as I can cook them. You can chargrill them indoors, but they are at their most tantalisingly sweet and smoky from the barbecue. Fantastic with burgers and bangers on hot sunny days.

Tear the sleeves of the corn away and remove the strands of silk. Combine the lime juice, olive oil and plenty of salt and pepper in a bowl. Add the cobs and toss well, then set aside.

Light the barbecue whilst the corn is marinating. Once the coals are hot enough, grill the corn on all sides until slightly blackened, soft and caramelised all over.

Sprinkle the cobs with the cumin and cayenne pepper and drizzle with either a little sour cream or mayonnaise, as you prefer.

WHY NOT TRY? These are also delicious tossed in chipotle butter. Mash up 2 tablespoons of Chipotles en adobo (page 238) with 100g butter and smear all over the corn once it has cooked. The smoky fieriness of the chillies and the sweet grilled corn are perfect bedfellows.

Feeds a greedy 4
Time: 20 minutes

6 corn cobs
juice of 2 limes
4 tablespoons extra virgin olive oil
sea salt and freshly ground black pepper
freshly ground cumin and cayenne pepper, to sprinkle
drizzle of sour cream or mayonnaise, or both!

Esquites

Esquites (ess-kee-tes) is a light, delicate broth bursting with fresh herb flavour and packed with buttery sweetcorn that has been simmered in it until tender, then heaped with goodies – chilli powder, crema (a slightly sour, thick Mexican cream) or mayo, totopos and a squeeze of fresh lime at the end. It is one of the most enticing street foods in Mexico, served in polystyrene cups to eat at any time of day. It is pretty healthy too, if you overlook the sour cream. At Wahaca we simmer our stock for 40 minutes with tarragon, mint and epazote, and when British corn is out of season, we use frozen. This is because freezing arrests the process of sugars turning to starch, and keeps the corn tasting as though it were picked yesterday. Serve as a starter, or enjoy as a satisfying meal in itself.

Heat a casserole over a medium flame and add the butter and oil. When the fats are sizzling, add the onion, salt, chilli and all the herbs save the mint. Cook over a medium heat for 10 minutes, until the onions have started to soften, then add the garlic. Continue to cook for a good 10 –15 minutes more. The longer you can sweat the onions and herbs at this stage, the more flavour the soup will have at the end of cooking. Finally, add the corn and mint, stir well and pour in the water or vegetable stock.

Simmer the whole mixture gently for 15–20 minutes to allow all the flavours to mingle and get to know each other. Add the lime juice and taste for seasoning; if you have used water or a homemade stock you will probably have to add a generous amount of salt and plenty of freshly ground black pepper.

Serve the esquites with spoonfuls of sour cream or crème fraîche, a touch of chilli powder, wedges of lime on the table, grated or crumbled cheese and a handful of Totopos, the Mexican equivalent of croutons, in each bowl.

Feeds 4–6 as a main course
Time: 1 hour

large knob of butter
3 tablespoons extra virgin olive oil
2 medium white onions, finely chopped
fine sea salt
1 green chilli, finely chopped
1 tablespoon dried epazote, or 2 tablespoons finely chopped fresh coriander root or stalks
small of fresh oregano or thyme, or 1 teaspoon dried oregano, preferably Mexican
3 bay leaves, preferably fresh
5 garlic cloves, finely chopped
1kg sweetcorn kernels (fresh or frozen)
a large handful of mint, finely chopped
1 litre water or vegetable stock
juice of 1 lime
freshly ground black pepper

To serve:
sour cream or crème fraîche
chilli powder
lime wedges
Lancashire or young pecorino cheese
Totopos (page 50)

Fiery little chicken tostadas

Tostadas, crisp little bases of corn on which to heap all kinds of delectable toppings, make lovely summer starters. They are easy to prepare and you can fry the tortillas in advance and store them in an airtight tin for up to a week. For informal eating, just put a whole load of these out when your guests first arrive and let them munch away whilst you get on with cooking the main course. No one will mind how unprepared you are with the rest of the food if they have something this tasty to tuck into first, especially if you offer them a cheeky glass of tequila as well.

First of all, get the tostadas made. Heat about 200ml of oil in a shallow frying pan until it is sizzling hot (you can test it with a piece of off-cut tortilla – the oil should really sizzle when it goes in). Cut each tortilla with a pastry cutter into 8cm rounds and fry them in the hot oil until crispy and golden. Drain on kitchen paper and sprinkle with salt.

Cover the chipotle chillies in boiling water and soak for about 15 minutes, or until they have softened. If you don't like too much spice, remove the seeds. Finely chop them and add half to the mayonnaise along with half the chopped jalapeños and all the herbs. Season the mayo with salt, pepper and a good squeeze of lime juice, then add the torn chicken. Check the heat level and add the rest of the chipotles if you like.

Place the tostadas on a large plate. Put a little pile of shredded lettuce onto each tostada, then a heaped teaspoonful of the chicken mayo mix and finally a couple of avocado slices and a little of the remaining pickled jalapeños. Be careful, you may find these addictive!

NOTE: To poach chicken breasts, place them in a small pan of salted boiling water with a few bay leaves, some peppercorns and a few slices of raw onion. Simmer very gently for no more than 15 minutes, until tender but not overcooked.

Feeds 4
Time: 30 minutes

sunflower oil, for frying corn tortillas
2 poached chicken breasts (see Note) or 400g leftover cooked chicken, torn into pieces
2 dried chipotle chillies
1 tablespoon pickled jalapeño slices, chopped
4 tablespoons homemade or Hellmann's mayonnaise
sea salt and freshly ground black pepper
small handful of chervil or tarragon or both
juice of 1 lime
4 leaves of baby gem lettuce, finely shredded
1 Hass avocado, roughly sliced into small pieces

How to eat a taco

I wouldn't want you to think the Mexicans have rules for everything but at Wahaca we like to think there is a code by which you eat tacos. Think of it as an insider's guide to the do's and don'ts of taco eating that will save face when in Mexico and have you eating like a native.

TACO DON'TS

Don't use a knife and fork.

Don't eat alone. If you are on your own, make friends with the person next to you because Mexican food is made for sharing.

TACO DO'S

Do make sure you have plenty of napkins around – Mexican food is messy stuff.

Do help yourself to salsa on the table, but don't dip food into it – lavish it onto your food instead.

Do tuck in if a plate of food is put in front of you with a basket of hot tortillas – it's a crime to let them get cold.

Do make sure you carefully wrap up the tortillas after helping yourself or your dining companions will complain. There is nothing worse than a cold tortilla.

Do share with friends (if you can bear to).

Summery spinach and feta tacos

When you order a taco from a street stand in Mexico, great bowls of fillings are lined up for you to pick from and you'll always find some kind of chard, spinach , courgette flower or wild green dish studded with fresh herbs and corn, tasting fresh and bursting with goodness. Yum! This makes a corker of a vegetarian dish, or serve it alongside a collection of other taco fillings. It is particularly good with a smoky salsa (page 233).

Heat a heavy-bottomed frying pan over a high heat and when it is smoking hot add the oil. Turn the heat to medium and throw in the onion, cumin, chilli, thyme and fresh corn. Fry, stirring, for about 10 minutes, until the corn is lightly coloured and the onion is soft. If you are using frozen corn, add this after the onion has softened. Season to taste with salt and pepper and add the garlic, cooking for a few minutes longer, before stirring in the tomatoes and spinach.

Stir the mixture for another few minutes to prevent anything catching before adding the herbs and lime juice. Check for seasoning again, adding more salt and pepper if needed. At this stage, the mixture can be cooled down and kept for later (it will last a few days in the fridge).

When you are ready to eat, warm through the spinach and corn, quickly toast the tortillas on each side and fill with the mixture. Crumble over the feta and serve with your favourite table salsas and, if you are being really Mexican, some little bowls of lime wedges and freshly chopped coriander.

Feeds 6–8
Time: 30 minutes

2 tablespoons olive oil
½ Spanish onion, finely diced
½ teaspoon ground cumin
1 jalapeño chilli, de-seeded and finely diced
2 teaspoons fresh thyme leaves or ½ teaspoon dried thyme
2 corn cobs, kernels removed, or about 265g frozen sweetcorn
sea salt and freshly ground black pepper
2 garlic cloves, crushed
2 large plum tomatoes, peeled, seeds removed and diced into small cubes
1 large bag of spinach, cooked and squeezed of excess water
small bunch of tarragon leaves, chopped
small handful of mint leaves, chopped
juice of ½ a lime

To serve:
warm corn tortillas
50g feta cheese
lime wedges
freshly chopped coriander

Rajas tacos

This classic filling is yet another example of how well the Mexicans cook vegetables. The word 'rajas' refers to strips of poblano chillies, which are available in the UK, either fresh from good greengrocers, or tinned from specialist shops, or from chilli stands at farmers' markets. The combination of the charred poblanos with slow-cooked onions, garlic and crème fraîche is a kind of ambrosia and works beautifully ladled over a savoury corn bread, as a sauce for steamed or baked fish, or served inside a good old jacket potato. These come on and off our menu at Wahaca, depending on the time of year, and have always been incredibly popular.

Heat a large, heavy-bottomed frying pan over a medium heat and when it is hot add the oil. Turn the heat to medium-low, add the onions, season well with salt and pepper and sweat for 10–15 minutes, until they turn into a silky, soft pile.

In the meantime, roast the poblanos directly over a gas flame, turning them from time to time, until they are blackened all over. Remove the stems, open the chillies out and, with a large chopping knife, scrape the seeds off one side and the blackened skin from the other (to make this easier you can let them cool first for 10 minutes in a clingfilm-wrapped bowl, but I don't always bother). Tear the chillies into strips and add to the onions with the garlic. Cook for another 10 minutes so that the flavour of the poblanos sinks into the onions, then add the crème fraîche. Check for seasoning and add the allspice, oregano and bay leaves. Simmer gently for 10 minutes to give the flavours a chance to meld.

Serve in hot tortillas, topped with a little grated cheese as a starter, or with a handful of other dishes and table salsas to share.

TIP: If you can't get hold of poblanos, flame-roast 3 green peppers and 1 or 2 green chillies instead.

Feeds 6–8
Time: 35 minutes

6 tablespoons olive oil
2 white onions, finely sliced
sea salt and freshly ground
    black pepper
3 poblano chillies
3 garlic cloves, finely chopped
250ml crème fraîche
good pinch of allspice
good pinch of dried oregano
2–3 bay leaves

To serve:
hot corn or flour tortillas
80g Wensleydale or Lancashire
    cheese

Steak & cheese tacos

Although the steak in this recipe is marinated for a few hours, the actual cooking takes only about ten minutes, making it excellent fast food – great for when you have friends over. Skirt is a very popular cut of steak in Mexico, as it costs so little but has a wonderfully rich flavour. Alternatively, buy some fillet or sirloin steak, or ask your butcher what cheap cuts he recommends.

If the skirt steak is cut into thick slices, butterfly it into thin steaks by cutting it through the middle with a sharp knife.

Put the peppercorns, oregano, salt and garlic in a pestle and mortar and bash together. Thin down with the orange and lime juice, then spread this mixture over the steaks. Cover and leave to marinate at room temperature for 30 minutes, or for a few hours in the fridge.

Remove the steak from the fridge at least 30 minutes before you cook it to bring it to room temperature. Heat a large, heavy-bottomed frying pan or griddle pan over a high heat. When it is smoking hot, add 2 tablespoons of the oil. Pat the steak dry with kitchen paper, then place in the pan and sear for 1–3 minutes a side, depending on the thickness of the steak. It needs to be pink and juicy in the midde or it will be tough to eat. You can test the steak for readiness by pressing it: it should be fairly giving when medium rare. Alternatively, transfer to a chopping board when you think it is done, allow to rest for 3–4 minutes, then cut into it. If it is still too bloody, just cook it for another minute or so.

Feeds 6–8
Time: 10 minutes + at least 30 minutes marinating

350g skirt steak
3 tablespoons olive oil
4 spring onions, chopped into pieces 3–3 cm long, then halved lengthways

For the marinade:
½ teaspoon black peppercorns
good pinch of dried oregano, preferably Mexican
good few pinches of sea salt
2 garlic cloves
juice of ½ an orange
juice of 1 lime

To serve:
corn or flour tortillas
Guacamole (page 194)
Cheddar cheese, grated
Refried beans (page 148, optional)

Whilst the steak is resting, add the remaining tablespoon of oil to the pan and fry the spring onions until they are soft and slightly charred, a few minutes.

Cut the steak into thin slivers across the grain. To do this, just look for the way the 'threads' run and cut against them rather than along them. This will improve the texture of the meat.

Wipe out the pan and quickly toast the tortillas on each side. Wrap in a napkin and place in a basket to keep them warm. Serve with bowls of table salsa, guacamole and cheese, and refried beans if you have them, then let everyone make their own tacos.

If you like, grill little piles of the grated Cheddar until they have melted and browned and hand them aound.

Crispy prawn taquitos with spicy avocado salsa

We tried something similar to these taquitos on our most recent staff trip to Mexico, outside the San Juan food market in Mexico City. I wondered then how such an apparently simple dish could be quite so sensational. The secret, it turns out, is in the awesome combination of flavours, which I think is often the way with Mexican food.

First make the garlic butter. Smash the head of garlic open with a jar or rolling pin and bash each clove to release the papery peel. Discard the peel, put the garlic and water in small blender and whiz together. Heat the butter until it is foaming, add the garlic purée and cook for 5–10 minutes, until most of the water has evaporated.

Meanwhile, quarter the tomatoes, scoop out the seeds (you can always save these for a tomato sauce), then cut the flesh into small dice. Heat the olive oil in a large frying pan and, when it is hot, add the onion and oregano. Cook for 5 minutes, until softened, seasoning well with salt and pepper. Add the chillies and two-thirds of the tomatoes, reserving the rest for the salsa, and continue to cook until almost all the moisture has evaporated. Turn the heat up, add the prawns and cook for a few minutes, until they have turned from grey to pink. If you can get only cooked prawns, simply heat them through in the sauce for a minute. Remove from the heat, stir in 1 tablespoon of the garlic butter and allow to cool.

Now make the salsa. Toss the remaining tomatoes with the diced avocado and onion and season to taste with the lime juice, jalapeños, coriander, salt and pepper…

Makes 6–8 taquitos
Time: 40 minutes

6 large plum tomatoes
4 tablespoons olive oil
1 onion, finely chopped
good pinch of dried oregano, preferably Mexican
sea salt and freshly ground black pepper
3 tablespoons finely chopped, pickled jalapeño chillies
300g sustainably caught raw prawns, chopped, or cooked prawns if you must
sunflower oil, for frying
6–8 flour tortillas
homemade or Hellmann's mayonnaise, to serve

For the garlic butter:
1 head of garlic
200ml water
60g butter

For the avocado and jalapeño salsa:
1 ripe Hass avocado, finely diced
½ red onion, chopped
juice of 1 lime
1 tablespoon pickled jalapeño chillies
small bunch of coriander, chopped

NOTE: You will need wooden toothpicks.

Heat the sunflower oil in a medium pan and, when warm, briefly dip each tortilla in to blanch. Fill one half of each tortilla with 2–3 tablespoons of the prawn mix, leaving 1cm of space all around, then fold over into a half-moon shape and 'pin' together with a couple of toothpicks (see diagrams). Turn the heat up and when the oil is sizzling hot, deep-fry the tortillas until they are golden and crispy, turning with tongs to cook both sides. Remove from the oil and drain on kitchen paper, removing the toothpicks.

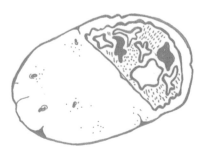

PLACE THE FILLING ON ONE HALF OF THE TORTILLA ...

Break open the taquitos and lay them out on a large serving dish. Spoon over dollops of salsa and mayonnaise and let everyone pile in.

WHY NOT TRY? For an easier treat, simply cut out rounds of tortilla about 4–5cm across and fry until crisp and golden (to make tostadas). Serve spread with a little mayonnaise, the prawn filling and then the avocado salsa on top. The garlic butter keeps for a week in the fridge and is delicious over all sorts of hot food.

FOLD IT OVER ...

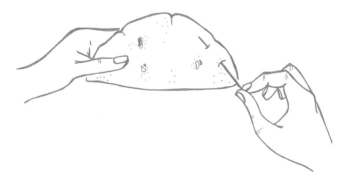

PIN SECURELY WITH TOOTHPICKS TO STOP THE FILLING ESCAPING

Crispy potato taquitos

The star of the show here is the habañero salsa, which we spent six months refining at Wahaca. Our food buyer Carolyn and I visited a cooperative of chilli farmers in the Yucatán, home to the habañero chilli. Tasting the most incredible salsas made with these exquisitely fruity, fiery, chillies in the local cantinas, we discovered that they work terrifically with seafood, but really stand out with the simple flavours of black beans and potatoes. These taquitos are exceedingly good, easy to make and, what's more, cost very little.

Cut the potatoes into equal-sized pieces and throw into a medium-sized saucepan. Cover with water, add a dash of salt and bring to the boil, cooking the pieces until they are tender. Meanwhile, finely chop the onions and jalapeños. When the potatoes are done, drain them and roughly dice. I like to keep the skin on.

Heat a large frying pan over a medium flame and when it is hot add the olive oil. Add the onions and chillies, season with salt and pepper and sweat until the onions are soft and translucent. Lower the heat and add the potatoes. Cook everything together for about 3 minutes, stirring to prevent sticking. The mixture should be fairly dry. Remove from the heat and stir in the Lancashire cheese and the lime juice. Season to taste with salt and pepper.

Pour the sunflower oil into a medium pan and heat until it is sizzling hot. Briefly dip each tortilla into the oil to blanch (this makes it easier to fold without breaking). Spoon 2–3 generous tablespoons of filling into each and fold over into a half-moon shape, 'pinning' the wrap together with a couple of toothpicks (see diagrams opposite).

Deep-fry the tortillas until they are golden and crispy, turning with tongs to cook both sides. Remove from the oil and drain on kitchen paper, removing the toothpicks. Serve topped with the lettuce, tomatoes and spring onions and drizzle over some sour cream and the fiery salsa.

Makes at least 8 taquitos
Time: 40 minutes

650g new potatoes, scrubbed
sea salt and freshly ground
    black pepper
2 medium onions
2–3 jalapeño chillies
5 tablespoons extra virgin
    olive oil
200g Lancashire cheese,
    crumbled
juice of 1 lime
sunflower oil, for frying
corn or flour tortillas

To serve:
2 baby gem lettuces, finely
    shredded
2 tomatoes, diced
2 spring onions, finely chopped
sour cream
Fruity, fiery salsa (page 240)

NOTE: You will need wooden toothpicks.

Broad bean, pea and new potato quesadilla

This is one of our favourite recipes at Wahaca. It is adapted from a breakfast I once had at a speciality bean market in a little town outside Mexico City. The broad beans were cooked, puréed and stuffed into variously shaped corn parcels, then griddled and drizzled with salsas, crema and lettuce. Served in quesadillas, our version is light, fresh, easy to make and tastes vibrantly of the summer.

Steam or cook the potatoes in salted, boiling water until they are tender, then drain and set aside. Heat a heavy-bottomed frying pan over a high heat and when it is hot add 3 tablespoons of olive oil. Turn the heat to medium, throw in the onion, garlic and chilli and cook for around 10 minutes, until the onion has softened. Meanwhile, bring a medium pan of salted water to the boil, add the broad beans and cook for about 3 minutes before adding the peas. Cook for a further 3–4 minutes, until the legumes are just tender.

With the back of a fork, gently mash the potatoes into the onion mix, seasoning with the lime juice, salt and pepper – bearing in mind that the feta is already salty. With your fork, gently fold in the rest of the olive oil, the peas, beans, herbs and feta. If the mixture looks dry, add another good glug of extra virgin olive oil.

Roughly spread a heaped tablespoonful of the mixture onto one half of each tortilla and sprinkle with the Cheddar. Fold the tortillas over into half-moon shapes, pressing the halves firmly together.

Heat a frying pan or griddle pan, brush the quesadillas with olive oil on both sides and cook until golden and crisp on each side, and warmed through.

Cut each quesadilla into 3 wedges and serve with your choice of salsas and ice-cold beer or fresh limeade and Agua frescas (page 202).

Feeds 2–4
Time: 40 minutes

225g new potatoes
5 tablespoons olive oil, plus extra for brushing
1 medium onion, finely chopped
2 garlic cloves, crushed
1 green chilli, de-seeded and finely chopped
200g frozen broad beans
100g frozen petit pois
juice of 1 lime
sea salt and freshly ground black pepper
small handful each of mint and tarragon leaves, finely chopped
45g feta cheese, crumbled
flour tortillas
80g Cheddar cheese, grated

Truffly mushroom quesadilla

One of the most popular street foods on our winter menu is the huitlacoche (wheat-la-coch-ay) quesadilla. Huitlacoche is an amazing ingredient – a pale blue-grey fungus that grows on corn, which turns a dark, inky black when cooked. In Mexico it is an expensive delicacy, prized for its intensely earthy, truffle-like flavour. When I can't find it tinned over here, I make quesadillas with mushrooms and truffle oil and think of Mexico. These are dead easy and deeelicious!

Heat a heavy-bottomed saucepan and when it is hot add a tablespoon of olive oil and the butter. Turn the heat to medium and, once the butter has melted, add the onion, garlic, as much chilli as you like and the oregano and cook for 5 minutes or until the onion has softened. Add the Portobellos, season with salt and pepper and cook for a further 5 minutes. Strain the dried mushrooms, reserving the liquid, then roughly chop and add them to the pan with half the reserved liquid. Carry on cooking until the liquid has almost evaporated.

Remove from the heat and add the parsley and truffle oil. Check for seasoning and add a little more truffle oil if you like. Mix the 2 cheeses together in a small bowl and set aside.

Roughly spread a heaped tablespoon of the mushroom mixture onto one half of each tortilla, then top with the cheese and the rocket (if you like). Fold the tortillas over into half-moon shapes, pressing the halves firmly together.

Heat a frying pan or griddle pan, brush the quesadillas with olive oil on both sides and cook until golden and crisp on each side, and warmed through

Cut each quesadilla into 3 wedges and serve with a rocket salad as a light starter, or as a tasty snack with drinks.

Feeds 4–6
Time: 35 minutes

olive oil
large knob of butter
1 red onion, finely sliced
1 large garlic clove, crushed
1 chile de árbol (preferably) or peperoncino, chopped, or pinch of chilli flakes
good pinch of dried oregano, preferably Mexican
8 large Portobello mushrooms, sliced
sea salt and freshly ground black pepper
20g dried porcini mushrooms, soaked in boiling water for 15 minutes
2 tablespoons roughly chopped flat leaf parsley,
6–8 drops of truffle oil
150g mozzarella cheese, grated
50g Cheddar cheese, grated
corn or flour tortillas

Empanadas: Mexican Pasties

Not many people know this but in the 19th century a whole lot of Cornish miners emigrated to Hidalgo in central Mexico to work the silver mines there. With them they took a quaint game that involved men kicking a ball around to one another. The Mexicans loved it – thus did football arrive in the Americas.

The newcomers also took their recipe for Cornish pasties, and it seems they caught on in a big way. The state of Hidalgo is still famous for its 'pastes', as they are known locally, and some of them are uncannily similar to the Cornish variety.

Is there a Cornish influence in the empanadas you find throughout North, Central and South America? I'd like to think so, though the best I ever tasted was filled with the decidedly Mexican ingredients of shredded chicken, fresh epazote and a wonderful light yellow mole. If I can't find that in London, I make do with a cheese and onion one! Fill your own with whatever you fancy and enjoy the mix!

Black bean and chorizo empanadas

Empanadas are a flaky rough pastry filled with any of the usual street food fillings and fried or baked until puffed up and crispy. Leo, one of our Superchefs at Wahaca, made the most amazing sweet potato ones at work which were the inspiration behind these. They are utterly scrumptious; start preparing them when you get peckish mid-morning and they will be ready on your plates, for lunch.

Preheat the oven to 200°C/390°F/gas 6. Meanwhile, make the pastry (or use ready-made puff pastry if you prefer). Sift the flour and salt into a large bowl, then rub in the lard until the mixture resembles large breadcrumbs. The less you work the pastry, the better. Mix the egg and water together, pour into the flour mix and stir with a fork until it just comes together. The dough will be soft, rough-textured and quite sticky. Gather it together with cool hands, sprinkle with flour and pat down to a thickness of 2–3cm. Cover with clingfilm and chill for at least 2 hours.

Meanwhile, dice the chorizo into 5mm chunks and put them in a large, heavy-bottomed frying pan over a medium-high heat. When the chorizo starts to release its fat, stir in the onion. Turn the heat down a little and cook the mixture until the onion has softened and turned translucent, about 10 minutes. Stir in the black beans, then mash so that they roughly bind everything together. Add the chopped thyme and remove from heat.

Divide the dough in 2 and, on a flour-dusted board, roll each half into a rectangle about 5mm thick. Cut each rectangle into 4 squares and transfer to oiled baking sheets. Cover with clingfilm and chill for 20 minutes. Put 1–2 generous tablespoonfuls of the chorizo mixture in the middle of each square. Brush some egg wash around the filling, then fold a corner of the pastry over to the opposite corner to make a triangle. Press the edges together with a fork. Brush the parcels with the remaining egg wash and prick with the fork once or twice to create air holes. Bake for 20 minutes, or until crisp and golden, turning over once during the cooking. Eat straight away.

Makes 8
Time: 35 minutes + 2½ hours chilling

400g cooked black beans, tinned or homemade (see page 148) – they should be cooked or heated until falling apart, then drained
250g good-quality chorizo, skin removed
1 medium onion, finely chopped
small handful of thyme, chopped
egg wash (1 egg mixed with a splash of milk)

For the pastry:
360g plain flour, chilled, plus extra for sprinkling
few good teaspoons salt
180g lard, chilled and cut into small cubes
1 egg
150ml ice-cold water

El pulpo

lighter dishes

in the c

CANTINA

PUDDINGS

PLATOS FUERTES

cantina

Lunch in Mexico is the big meal of the day. It starts at two or three in the afternoon and lasts a good few hours, sometimes even stretching into the night. And to eat it in style, there is only one place to go: **the cantina!**

**M**arkets are our inspiration, but when it came to designing Wahaca, we went for a cantina style: relaxed, informal, vibrant and bustling. In Mexico, the cantina is a place where anyone can drop in at any time of the day for a quick snack and a drink, a leisurely feast with friends, or a few tacos mid-shop. There is a saying in Mexico that important decisions are always made over lunch – and the cantina is a great place to talk shop and do business. Where better to hold difficult discussions and complex negotiations than around a table with good food, good wine and possibly even tequila?

Cantinas can be little more than barely decorated rooms on the side of the road, where the menu of the day is served with no choice but always a minimum of three courses, leaving one happy and replete. You can expect to pay very little, but the food will be first class and the kitchens clean. More upmarket establishments offer a much wider range of dishes, allowing you to choose from dozens of nibbles, starters, main courses and puddings. These menus are tricky for those with big appetites. It is all too easy to get carried away with the ordering, indulge your every craving and then roll out several hours later feeling substantially heavier. Pacing oneself is key!

What I find appealing about these long lunches is their tempo. Courses come in a designated order, appearing one after the other in a continuous rhythm of abundance and generosity. First come cooling jugs of Agua fresca (page 202) or, if you are drinking, perhaps a small glass of tequila with a spicy Sangrita (page 210). Ice-cold beer might follow with plates of antojitos (an-toh-hee-toss), or 'little treats', the equivalent of Italian antipasti.

Then comes the soup course, whether a 'dry' soup (page 102) or a more recognisable 'wet' soup. Or you could opt for pasta, which is surprisingly common in Mexico, or cheese melted with some delicious sauce and scooped onto warm tortillas or a plate of quesadillas. Ceviches and salpicóns (warm seafood salads) are also popular. In fact, salads are increasingly fashionable in Mexico, particularly amongst those who watch their waistline. After these 'lighter' dishes come the hearty platos fuertes: main courses of delicious thick moles, hearty braises, baked fish, grilled fish or seafood. Finally, there is pudding, and the people really go to town here (pages 154–75).

Mexicans know that food and company go hand in hand, and the best way to celebrate this is with a lunch fit for a king.

MOUTH-WATERING...

soups &

Traditional recipes vary from region to region in Mexico, inspired by local ingredients – including chillies, wild mushrooms and tender greens or quelites (keh-lee-tez) – many of which grow in only one area within a state. The remarkably fresh-tasting Sopa de guia (page 80), for example, is made from all parts of the courgette plant, plus white corn and the indigenous herbs chepil and hierba de conejo, so an 'authentic' version is virtually impossible to recreate outside Oaxaca.

The inaccessibility of key ingredients created some stumbling blocks when we first opened Wahaca. But having settled on the kind of street food we wanted to do, we educated suppliers so that we could get the dried chillies we needed, and bought whole crates full of ingredients such as mole, huitlacoche and cactus when nobody else was using them. When sourcing fresh fish, dairy and herbs, we gave ourselves the freedom to substitute local ingredients with similar characteristics and flavour profiles. And we worked hard to make the most of ingredients that were available.

Resourcefulness is something the Mexicans understand. Since most cooks

ZINGY TOMATOES

salads

AND SUPER HEALTHY

wouldn't dream of throwing out anything that might add sustenance to the next meal, homemade stocks are used in every soup, flavoured from bones, herbs and the tops and tails of fresh vegetables. This is real cooking, where whole meals are whipped up from a few scraps, the way we used to cook in Britain before we embraced the culture of ready meals and decided that leftovers were not worth our while.

To make these soups nourishing, elegant and even more mouth-watering, they are garnished with a range of ingredients that add texture, bite and body: deep-fried strips of tortilla, chunks of silky avocado, fried chillies, crumbled cheese, fresh lime and chopped coriander. Each soup has its own

garnish that brings out or complements its core flavour.

Salads are similarly full of taste and texture and the most exciting ingredients. Ensalada de nopal or Cactus salad (page 89) dates back centuries, whilst more modern incarnations take influences from the European conquistadores. Thus beetroot, goats' cheese and walnuts are often found together, alongside fresh cheese and avocado. The most famous of them all is the Caesar salad (page 90), actually invented in Mexico in the last century and now replicated across the globe. Who knew that Mexico had so much influence?

Black bean soup

There is something unfailingly comforting about black bean soup. It warms the soul and makes life feel good, particularly when cooked with a touch of chilli and served drizzled with sour cream and crumbled feta cheese.

Heat a heavy-bottomed frying pan and dry-roast the tomatoes and garlic (see page 234).

Meanwhile, heat the butter and a tablespoon of oil in a large, heavy-bottomed pan and when it is gently foaming add the onion and herbs. Sweat for about 5–10 minutes, until the onion is soft, then add the garlic. Cook for another few minutes before adding the tomatoes and Chipotles en adobo, if using, seasoning well with salt and pepper. Cook gently for a few minutes before adding the beans (and their cooking liquid if you made your own). Cook a little longer before adding the stock and lime juice, then simmer gently for 10–15 minutes so that the flavours can develop.

Whiz briefly with a stick blender for a textured soup with a bit of bite, or purée until smooth. Pour the soup into 6 warm bowls and scatter over the feta, salsa and coriander and spoon over a dollop of sour cream.

WHY NOT TRY? Omit the Fresh tomato salsa and serve with sour cream and some deep-fried ancho chillies (page 85) for a more exotic flavour.

Feeds 6
Time: 35 minutes

2 plum tomatoes
3 garlic cloves, unpeeled
25g butter or lard
olive oil
½ white onion, finely chopped
1–2 tablespoons chopped fresh
    oregano or marjoram,
    or 1 teaspoon dried oregano
2 fresh bay leaves
1–2 teaspoons Chipotles en
    adobo (page 78, optional)
sea salt and freshly ground
    black pepper
600g cooked black beans,
    tinned or homemade (see
    page 148)
800–1000ml chicken or
    vegetable stock
juice of 1 lime

To serve:
100g feta cheese, crumbled
100g Fresh tomato salsa
    (page 232)
small handful of coriander,
    chopped
sour cream

Sopa de guía

Sopa de guía is the cleanest, most delicate-tasting soup you will ever come across and is made almost exclusively in the state of Oaxaca from different parts of the courgette plant and wild herbs. This is my version, made with ingredients that you can buy in the UK, and I think it does the original justice. It is absurdly good for you, and especially delicious when drizzled with a little chile de árbol oil at the end. It would make a swanky starter, a comforting supper or simply the perfect detox. How's that for one recipe?

If you can get hold of the chard, shred the leaves and cut the stems into 5cm pieces. Open out the courgette flowers, if using), discard their stamens and tear each flower into 3 or 4 pieces.

Heat a large, heavy-bottomed pan and add 2 tablespoons of olive oil. Turn the heat to medium-low, add the onion and garlic and cook gently for 2–3 minutes. Add the celery, thyme and/or oregano and cook for a further 3 minutes. Add the corn, chard stems and sliced courgettes and pour in the stock. Bring to the boil, then simmer gently until the courgettes are cooked, around 3–4 minutes. Add the chard leaves, simmer for another minute, then add the spring onions, chervil, spinach and courgette flowers (if using): these should all gently wilt into the other vegetables.

If you prefer, you can liquidise this soup but I love the clear broth with all the greens floating in it; it looks so pretty as it is. Best served straight away with drizzles of Chile de árbol oil and, if you like, some fried tortilla strips and a touch of grated pecorino.

NOTE: If you grow your own courgettes, you will have plenty of flowers. If not, you can find them in good greengrocers. Even without them, you will still have the most brilliant soup.

Feeds 4
Time: about 30 minutes

200g Swiss chard (optional)
4 small courgettes, finely diced, plus 4 courgette flowers (optional)
extra virgin olive oil
1 white onion, finely chopped
2 garlic cloves, crushed
2 sticks of celery, finely chopped (add the leaves as well, they are full of flavour and look pretty)
small bunch of thyme and/or oregano leaves, chopped
1 corn cob, kernels removed, or about 200g frozen sweetcorn
600ml chicken or vegetable) stock
4 spring onions, finely sliced
small bunch of chervil or tarragon, finely chopped
200g baby spinach

To serve:
Chile de árbol oil (page 237)
fried tortilla strips (optional)
grated pecorino cheese (optional)

Grilled corn soup

In September, when corn is in season in the UK, standing proud in the fields, I like to make this soup and serve it either very hot or very cold, depending on the weather. Despite being so simple, it is a real crowd-pleaser with a stand-out, deep flavour thanks to the grilling. The recipe also works really well with barbecued corn.

Preheat the grill. Brush the corn cobs with a little olive oil, then place them on a foil-covered baking sheet and gently grill, turning often until the kernels start to colour. Cool slightly, then slice the kernels off the cobs.

Heat 2 tablespoons of olive oil in a medium saucepan. Add the onions, garlic and cumin and cook until soft and translucent. Add the chilli, salt and pepper and a pinch of sugar, and cook for a further 2–3 minutes. Add the grilled corn kernels and the chicken stock, bring to the boil, then simmer for 5 minutes. Remove from the heat and whiz until smooth with a stick blender. Stir in the lime juice and season again if necessary.

Garnish each serving with a dollop of sour cream and a sprinkling of chopped herbs.

WHY NOT TRY? For an alternative garnish, add a dollop of chipotle cream, made by mixing sour cream with a little chipotle paste, some salt, pepper and a squeeze of lime juice.

Feeds 4
Time: 30 minutes

5 corn cobs
2 tablespoons olive oil, plus
    a little more for brushing
2 small red onions, finely
    chopped
2 garlic cloves, crushed
pinch of ground cumin
1 red chilli, finely diced
sea salt and freshly ground
    black pepper
pinch of sugar
1 litre chicken stock
juice of 1 lime

To serve:
sour cream
small handful of coriander or
    chives, chopped

Lentil and plantain soup

The combination of earthy lentils and sweet plantain is an inspired one. Pia Quintana, a wonderful chef and a great friend, first told me about this soup a few years back. I have to admit, I didn't rush to try the recipe. What a mistake! This is soup is seriously good and a really economical, satisfying supper. The chile de árbol oil really brings it alive, so do make that if you can.

Drain the lentils and place in a saucepan. Cover with at least 5cm of water, adding a bashed garlic clove, 2 of the bay leaves and a few peppercorns (if you have half an onion or carrot lying around, add these too). Simmer for about 30 minutes, or until the lentils are completely soft, adding a good teaspoon of salt towards the end of cooking.

In the meantime, heat a heavy-bottomed frying pan and dry-roast the tomatoes for about 10–15 minutes, turning occasionally until they are thoroughly blackened and charred.

Meanwhile, heat a medium saucepan and add 3 tablespoons of olive oil. When the oil is sizzling, add the onion and cook over a medium-low heat until soft and translucent, about 10 minutes. Add the remaining garlic, finely chopped, half the plantain, the last bay leaf and the oregano. Season well with salt and pepper and a good pinch of the brown sugar. Turn the heat right up and cook, stirring from time to time to scrape up anything sticking to the bottom of the pan as the plantain caramelises.

Feeds 6
Time: 40 minutes + at least
   3–4 hours soaking

500g green lentils, soaked in
   water overnight, or for at least
   3–4 hours
4 garlic cloves
3 fresh bay leaves
few peppercorns
sea salt and freshly ground
   black pepper
2 large tomatoes, left whole
olive oil
1 medium onion, finely
   chopped
2 very ripe plantains, peeled
   and chopped into small
   chunks
2 teaspoons dried oregano
1 generous teaspoon soft
   brown sugar
juice of 1 lime
1 litre chicken stock
large bunch of fresh coriander,
   roots/stalks finely chopped,
   and leaves roughly chopped

To serve:
sour cream or crème fraîche
Chile de árbol oil (page 237)

When the mixture looks golden and is quite dry, add the tomatoes, breaking them up with a wooden spoon. Finally, add the lentils, lime juice and stock and simmer for 10–15 minutes, adding the finely chopped roots or stalks of the coriander.

When you're ready to eat, heat a little oil in a frying pan, add the remaining plantain and fry until it is golden and crispy all over, seasoning with the remaining sugar, plus salt and pepper. Check the soup for seasoning (lentils take quite a bit of salt) and serve with a dollop of crème fraîche, a drizzle of the chilli oil (if using) and a sprinkling of fried plantain and chopped coriander leaves.

Roast tomato tortilla soup

Don't be put off by the length of this recipe! It is the most popular soup in Mexico, and with all the wonderful garnishes you lay on the table, it can make a spectacular starter or lunch. If you can't get hold of every chilli, stick to the chipotle, or simply throw in a couple of fresh chillies and some smoked paprika instead. But if you can make the effort to find the guajillo and ancho chillies, it's worth it for the deep, intense flavour they provide.

If using fresh tomatoes, turn the grill to its highest setting and line a baking sheet with foil. Put the tomatoes under the grill and cook for about 15 minutes, turning occasionally until they are thoroughly blackened all round.

In the meantime, prepare the 3 types of chilli as described overleaf. Once they are toasted, soak in a bowl of boiling water for 15 minutes.

Now put the olive oil and onion into a frying pan and stir over a low heat. After 5 minutes, add the garlic and plenty of salt and pepper, cooking until the onion is translucent. Add the chopped herbs along with the tomatoes. Cook until the tomatoes start to fall apart, then add the chillies, drained of their soaking water, and the stock. Bring to the boil, then reduce the heat to a low simmer.

After the soup has simmered for another 5–10 minutes, whiz it up with a stick blender and season to taste. It may need more salt and a good pinch of brown sugar to bring out the flavour of the tomatoes. Ladle into hot bowls and serve at the table with bowls of the deep-fried anchos, sour cream, crispy totopos, coriander leaf, feta, avocado and lime wedges. This is a showstopper of a soup!

NOTE: To deep-fry chillies, heat about 5 cm oil in a small saucepan. Slice the chillies, place them on a metal slotted spoon and deep-fry for 5 seconds, until they puff up. Be careful not to burn them or they will be bitter.

Feeds 6
Time: 1 hour

4 large, ripe beef tomatoes (about 1kg) or 3 x 400g tins plum tomatoes
5 guajillo chillies (approx. 25g)
2 ancho chillies (approx. 25g)
1 chipotle chilli
4 tablespoons extra virgin olive oil
1 onion, finely chopped
3 garlic cloves, chopped
sea salt and freshly ground black pepper
large bunch of coriander, stems finely chopped and most of the leaves roughly chopped (save some whole leaves to garnish)
handful of oregano and thyme leaves, roughly chopped
1 litre chicken stock
pinch of brown sugar (optional)

To serve:
2 deep-fried ancho chillies (see Note)
150ml sour cream
Totopos (page 50), cut into thin little matchsticks
150g feta cheese, crumbled
2 avocados, diced at the last minute
lime wedges

Using dried chillies

There are hundreds of types of chillies in Mexico, many of which are dried which makes them easier to transport and allows them to be stored for ages. Chillies have an astonishing range of deep complex flavours. Here is how you cook with them…

1. Tear open the chillies, discarding the stem and seeds. (Sometimes you keep the seeds, but usually only when making a dark-coloured mole.)

2. Tear the chillies into flat pieces (roughly 4–5cm). You want them to lie flat and toast evenly, with every part of the skin in contact with the pan.

3. Heat a dry, heavy-bottomed frying pan over a medium-high heat. When hot, lay out a small handful of chilli pieces and toast them very briefly, just enough for them to soften and bend, become fragrant, slightly darken in colour and, in some cases, bubble up in parts. Be careful not to burn them! In toasting, you want to release the chillies' flavour, nothing more, so use your nose as you toast them and remove as soon as you think they are done, about 10–20 seconds a side. If they are toasting too quickly, turn the heat down a little. A burnt chilli will make a whole sauce taste bitter.

4. Soak the chillies in boiling water for 15–20 minutes or according to the recipe instructions. In most cases the recipe will not require you to use the chilli soaking water.

Avocado soup

Avocados are not only a treat; they are also bursting with good oils and vitamins, making them a bona fide super-food. This soup is rich, so you don't need huge bowlfuls, but so creamy that it is hard to stop eating. I serve it cold, although it is really good hot. Despite the gentle kick from the chilli, it tastes extraordinarily delicate and, with the best-quality avocados, makes a rather special starter.

Cut the tip off the chilli and taste it carefully. If it is very hot, remove the seeds; if not, leave them in and roughly chop. Halve and stone the avocados and scoop the flesh into a blender. Add the garlic and chilli and blend, gradually adding the chicken stock until smooth. Season with the lime juice, tequila, salt and pepper. Taste and add a dash of Tabasco if you like.

Chill the soup overnight, or for at least 2 hours.

Pour into bowls and either garnish with a dollop of sour cream and some chopped coriander, or serve with Fresh tomato salsa and totopos or ready-made tortilla chips.

Feeds 4
Time: 20 minutes + at least
   2 hours chilling

1 green chilli
4 ripe Hass avocados
1 garlic clove, crushed
1.2 litres chicken stock, chilled
juice of 1 lime
good dash of blanco tequila
   (optional)
sea salt and freshly ground
   black pepper
3–4 drops of Tabasco sauce
   (optional)

To serve:
sour cream and small handful
   of chopped coriander or
   chives
OR
Fresh tomato salsa (page 232)
   and Totopos (page 50) or
   ready-made tortilla chips

Avocado salad

This is the most delicious salad, with ripe avocado, crispy bacon, lettuce and toasted almonds all dressed in a thick, creamy avocado dressing. It makes a nutritious and amazingly tasty lunch.

First make the dressing. Whiz the avocado flesh and lime juice together in a blender and season with salt, pepper and a good pinch of sugar. Add the rest of the dressing ingredients and blend to a smooth liquid, thinning down with a little cold water if the texture is too thick.

Heat a frying pan over a medium heat and add the almonds. Toss them for about 5 minutes to lightly toast. Cool and roughly chop. Add a drizzle of sunflower oil to the pan and fry the pancetta until crisp before draining on kitchen paper.

Shred half the lettuce leaves and place in a large mixing bowl with half the avocado, half the chilli and spring onions, and 2–3 pieces of the crispy pancetta, crumbled. Add a large spoonful of the dressing, season with a little salt and pepper and toss together.

Lay out the remaining lettuce leaves on 4 plates and divide the salad between them. Spoon more dressing on top, followed by the remaining avocado, bacon, chilli, spring onions, coriander and almonds. Serve at once.

Feeds 4
Time: 25 minutes

small handful of almonds
sunflower oil, for frying
12 thin slices of pancetta or
  bacon
3 heads of baby gem lettuce
1 Hass avocado, roughly diced
1 green chilli, finely sliced (de-
  seeded if you want less heat)
2 spring onions, finely sliced
1 tablespoon roughly chopped
  coriander

For the dressing:
1 Hass avocado
juice of ½ a lime
sea salt and freshly ground
  black pepper
pinch of sugar
75ml extra virgin olive oil
1 heaped teaspoon Dijon
  mustard
2 spring onions, roughly
  chopped
small bunch of basil

Cactus Salad

You can buy tinned nopal (cactus) in specialist shops, and it really is worth trying. In Mexico it is well known for helping the digestive system, and is very popular in salads and juices for those on diets, although it must be said that it is also fantastic covered in cheese and grilled in tacos. I love its salty, meaty taste, brilliant with tomatoes in this light salad.

Whisk the dressing ingredients together and set aside.

In a large bowl, gently mix all the salad ingredients with the dressing, finishing with the grated cheese.

I love to serve this with Totopos (page 50), but that doesn't make it nearly so healthy!

Feeds 4
Time: 10 minutes

6 medium vine tomatoes, roughly chopped
1 x 175g tin cactus, drained, rinsed and roughly chopped
1 small red onion, finely sliced
small handful of curly parsley, finely chopped
small handful of coriander leaves, roughly chopped
50g pecorino cheese, grated

For the dressing:
60ml extra virgin olive oil
juice of 1 lime
pinch of caster sugar
sea salt and freshly ground pepper

Caesar salad

This salad was invented in Tijuana in 1924 by Caesar Cardini, a restaurateur faced with a full house and just a few unpromising ingredients – stale bread, anchovies and lettuce. Resourcefulness, a thoroughly Mexican trait, can make you a culinary star! This classic Caesar with chicken was on our menu when we first opened Wahaca.

Preheat oven to 170°C/335°F/gas 3.

Put the chicken pieces in a saucepan, cover with cold water and add the bay leaves, half a teaspoon of salt, some pepper and the onion. Bring to the boil, then turn the heat down so that the water is barely simmering. Cook for 10 minutes, then turn off the heat, allowing the pieces to cool in the liquid.

To make the dressing, put the egg yolks, lemon juice, mustard, anchovies and garlic into a blender or food processor. With the motor running, gradually add the olive oil, beginning with a very slow, thin stream to get the mayonnaise started. Blend to the consistency of double cream, then add the Parmesan cheese and the Worcestershire sauce – you might need to add a splash of water towards the end if the dressing gets too thick. Taste and season with salt and pepper, and don't be afraid to add more lemon juice if needed.

Cut the lettuce in half lengthways and break up the leaves. Wash and dry them, then put into a large salad bowl. Combine the olive oil, thyme, salt and pepper in a separate bowl and toss the bread in it. Transfer to a baking sheet and bake in the oven for 5–10 minutes, until golden and crispy. Meanwhile, drain the chicken, strip the flesh off in large chunks and add to the lettuce along with the diced avocados.

Season the salad leaves with salt and pepper, add the croutons, then pour over the dressing and gently toss. Scatter lovely big shavings of Parmesan over the top and serve straight away.

Feeds 4
Time: 45 minutes

8 chicken pieces
2 bay leaves
sea salt and freshly ground black pepper
1 small onion, quartered
head of cos lettuce
½ loaf of white crusty bread, torn into chunks
100ml olive oil
fresh thyme
2 Hass avocados, diced
80–100g Parmesan or pecorino cheese, shaved with a potato peeler

For the dressing:
2 egg yolks
juice of ½ a lemon
1 teaspoon Dijon mustard
6 sustainably caught anchovy fillets (check the label), chopped
1 small garlic clove, crushed
200ml olive oil
1-2 tablespoon grated Parmesan or Gran Padano cheese
dash of Worcestershire sauce

Green rice salad

When we first opened Wahaca and I was working in the kitchen, we would get very inventive with the ingredients on hand for staff meals. Our Mexican green rice (page 144) has always been a firm favourite, so I concocted a salad with it, using bits and pieces that were lying around. The result is comforting yet zingy, with a wonderful touch of fire thanks to the habañero chilli. It is now a firm favourite at home, though for speed I no longer make it with Mexican green rice. This salad is glorious on a sunny day with any barbecued food.

Whisk the dressing ingredients together and set aside.

Soak the rice in cold water for 20 minutes, then rinse well in a sieve. Place in a saucepan and cover with double the volume of water. Bring to the boil and simmer for about 15 minutes, or until the rice is just cooked but still has a light bite to it and has absorbed all the water. Season well with salt, pepper and 2–3 tablespoons of the dressing, then leave to cool (unless you want a warm salad, in which case cover it with foil or greaseproof paper and keep in a warm oven).

Meanwhile, place a large frying pan over a high heat and, when it is smoking hot, add the olive oil. After a minute, add the shallots, garlic, courgettes and corn. Stir-fry them over a high heat for 5–10 minutes, until the vegetables have taken a little colour and are just cooked through. You want them to keep their shape. Transfer to a large salad bowl to cool down.

Toss the vegetables and the rice with the tomatoes, spring onions, feta, lime juice and half of the chopped chilli. Add enough dressing for a moist but not too wet salad and check for seasoning. Finally, toss in the fresh herbs and the Totopos, and add the remaining chilli if you want the salad spicy.

Feeds 6–8
Time: 45 minutes

200g basmati rice
3 tablespoons extra virgin
   olive oil
4 small shallots, finely chopped
1 garlic clove, crushed
2 large courgettes, diced
2 corn cobs, kernels removed,
   or about 400g frozen
   sweetcorn
4 plum tomatoes, diced
3 spring onions, finely chopped
160g feta cheese, crumbled
juice of 1 lime
½ habañero or Scotch bonnet
   chilli, finely chopped
large handful each of mint
   and coriander, finely
   chopped
small handful of tarragon,
   finely chopped
Totopos (page 50), cut into thin
   little matchsticks

For the dressing:
60ml extra virgin olive oil
juice of 1 lime
pinch of caster sugar
sea salt and freshly ground
   pepper

Cucumber, chilli, beetroot and ricotta salad

When I first arrived in Mexico aged eighteen, I was amazed by how healthy much of the food was. Exploding the myth of a heavy, greasy cuisine, I found markets full of incredible fruit and vegetables, and smart cafés in Mexico City offering light salads bursting with fresh flavour. Both cucumber and beetroot are popular ingredients, not only in salads but in juices too. In this recipe, I've combined them with ricotta in place of requesón (Mexican curd cheese) to make a refreshing, light and creamy dish. If you can't get hold of chervil, use tarragon or basil, or both. This is the perfect side salad or starter, so good alongside a few other dishes for a summery feast.

Preheat the oven to 180°C/350°F/gas 4.

Scrub the beetroot clean and rub with a little olive oil, salt and pepper. Place in a baking tin and roast for 30–40 minutes, until they are tender when you pierce them with a knife. Don a pair of rubber gloves, slip off the beetroot skin and cut the flesh into small chunks.

Empty the ricotta into a bowl and, using a fork, beat in 3–4 tablespoons of the olive oil, the herbs, half the chilli and the garlic. Season with salt and pepper.

Cut the cucumber in half lengthways, scoop out the seeds using a teaspoon and slice the flesh into half-moons about 5mm thick.

Divide the lime juice, vinegar and remaining oil between 2 bowls. Toss the cucumber in one and the beetroot in the other. Season both.

Now spread the ricotta across a big plate. Place the beetroot on top of the ricotta, the cucumber on top of the beetroot and drizzle over a little extra virgin olive oil. Sprinkle with the remaining green chilli and bring to the table for everyone to tuck in.

Feeds 4–6
Time: 45 minutes

3–4 medium beetroot
100ml extra virgin olive oil, plus extra for rubbing/drizzling
sea salt and freshly ground black pepper
250g ricotta cheese
small handful of chervil, finely chopped
small handful of mint, finely chopped
1 green chilli, finely chopped
1 small garlic clove, crushed
1 large cucumber
juice of 1 lime
1–2 tablespoons red wine vinegar

Three-tomato salad

Ripe, succulent tomatoes go stunningly well with pineapples, which grow along the length of Mexico's Caribbean coast, tasting as juicy and sweet as mangoes. This is a simple yet seductive salad with vivid colour, a tangy sharpness and terrific taste: a real winner either as a starter or as part of an alfresco lunch.

Place all the dressing ingredients in a clean jam jar, put the lid on and shake vigorously to mix.

Peel the pineapple and cut lengthways into 4 wedges. Slice away the tough inner core, then cut 2 of the wedges widthways into thin slices. Keep the rest for breakfast or a tasty treat later.

Cut the cherry and baby tomatoes in half, quarter the bigger tomatoes and combine with all the fruit, gently tossing in the dressing. Scatter with the fresh herbs, crumble over the feta and season with salt and pepper. Serve on your prettiest plate.

Feeds 4
Time: about 20 minutes

1 small ripe pineapple
150g cherry tomatoes
150g baby yellow tomatoes
150g very ripe tomatoes (green, yellow or red)
small bunch of coriander, roughly torn
small handful of fresh marjoram or thyme leaves, roughly chopped
80g feta cheese
sea salt and freshly ground black pepper

For the dressing:
60ml extra virgin olive oil
1–2 tablespoons red wine vinegar
good pinch of caster sugar
sea salt and freshly ground pepper

SHARE...

lighter

OR BE SHELLFISH!

You can snack on many of the dishes in this section at the market, but the lovely thing about eating them in a cantina (or recreating them at home) is that you get to sit down and savour them.

dishes

The choice is certainly thrilling. Small bowls of pasta flavoured with dried chillies are sprinkled with aged cheeses that taste curiously similar to Italian pecorino. Ceviche (pages 104–6) is accompanied by piles of crackers and tortilla chips for scooping up the lime-drenched fish and balancing the heat of its chilli marinade. Queso fundido (page 112), the Mexican equivalent of cheese fondue, is brought to the table piping hot with a basket of freshly baked, steaming-hot flour tortillas.

This course hits the spot if you are the type of person who prefers *not* to share your food (you can order just enough for yourself). But it is also perfect for those who like to taste as much as possible. Order a bunch of items and you can happily share dishes with your friends and work your way around the menu.

Don't go too wild, though. It is all too easy to go the whole hog and eat too much. You need enough to satisfy certainly, but not so much as to spoil the course that follows.

Prawns enchipotlada

Once you have made the mojo, this is one of the fastest supper dishes you can make and it always goes down a treat. Garlicky chilli-doused prawns with masses of buttery juices – this is our kind of food.

Season the prawns. Put a large, heavy-bottomed frying pan over a high heat and, when it is smoking hot, add the oil. Once the oil is shimmering hot, throw in the prawns and cook for 2–3 minutes. Shake the pan to turn the prawns, then add the tequila, which may or may not catch light. After a few moments, add the mojo de ajo and the chipotle. Cook for another 30 seconds before adding the lime juice and butter. Heat through, simmer for 30 seconds and remove from heat.

Scatter in the coriander and serve at once with warm tortillas, rice or crusty bread. Deeeelicious!

Feeds 4–5
Time: 10 minutes

sea salt and freshly ground
  black pepper
450g sustainably caught,
  peeled prawns, uncooked
2 tablespoons olive or
  sunflower oil
2 tablespoons reposado tequila
3-4 tablespoons Mojo de ajo
  (page 229)
1 teaspoon Chipotles en adobo
  (page 238), or more if you
  want a fiery dish
juice of 1 lime
large knob of butter
handful of coriander, chopped
warm tortillas, rice or crusty
  bread, to serve

Crab salpicón

A salpicón is a salad that you can eat stuffed inside soft, warm tacos or ladled over crisp tostadas. It can be served cold but I love it warm and fiery, alive with the flavours of sweet crabmeat, fruity habañero and citrus. This makes a great starter but is just as good with rice for dinner.

Peel and finely chop the shallots and set aside. Trim and finely chop the fennel, discarding the tough outer layer. Cover the tomatoes with boiling water, leave for 20 seconds, then peel, quarter, de-seed and cut into 1cm dice. Finely chop the habañero and immediately scrub your hands to avoid putting chilli fingers anywhere near yourself or others!

Pour a generous 3–4 tablespoons of olive oil into a saucepan and put over a medium heat. Add the shallots and cook for a few minutes before throwing in the fennel, chilli and oregano. Season with salt and carry on cooking for another few minutes, until the fennel has softened a little. Now add the achiote paste (if using), citrus juices, crabmeat, tomatoes and coriander and gently heat through, another minute or so. Taste, adjust the seasoning and serve with crisp tostadas or warm tortillas on the side.

Feeds 6–8 as a starter
Time: 25 minutes

2 large banana shallots or
  5 small ones
1 fennel bulb
4 ripe plum tomatoes
½ habañero or Scotch bonnet
  chilli
extra virgin olive oil
small handful of oregano or
  thyme, finely chopped
sea salt and freshly ground
  black pepper
1 teaspoon achiote paste
  (see page 132) or chopped
  chipotles (optional)
juice of 2 limes
juice of 1 orange
3 dressed crabs (about 400g
  crabmeat)
small handful of coriander,
  roughly chopped
tostada (see page 54, step 1) or
  warm tortillas, to serve

Scallop and prawn aguachile

Enrique Olvera, a great chef from Mexico City, taught me the secrets of making aguachile (literally 'firewater') about seven years ago. This recipe is blissfully easy to prepare. Lime juice and chilli are blitzed together to make a beautifully refreshing seafood marinade. Served in small glasses or glass bowls, this makes a very swanky-looking little starter.

Prepare the scallops by slicing off the tough muscles that run along one side. Cut off the roe and save this to make a delicious salad topping fried with some bacon. Peel the prawns and use the tip of a sharp knife to remove the black vein that runs along the back. Rinse all the seafood and cut into 1cm dice.

Pour the lime juice into a blender, adding half the chilli, the fish sauce, salt, sugar and a 5cm chunk of the cucumber. Blitz the lot, pour in the tequila and taste for seasoning. Depending on the heat of your chilli, you might want to add the remaining half to the blender, or even add another one. You are looking for an extremely hot marinade, albeit one that you can actually taste. Add more fish sauce, salt or sugar if you think it needs it. You want a refreshing liquid that is not so sharp that it makes you suck your teeth. The tequila gives it an incredible flavour, so seeking out a good bottle is well worth the effort.

Transfer the marinade to a bowl. Add the shallot, cherry tomatoes and the seafood and mix together. Cut the rest of the cucumber in half lengthways, scoop out the seeds with a teaspoon and cut the flesh into slices about 5mm thick. Add to the bowl of marinade, then cover and put in the fridge for 1–4 hours so that the lime juice has a chance to 'cook' the seafood.

When you are ready to eat, roughly chop the herbs and stir most of these into the aguachile. Ladle modest servings into small bowls and top with the avocado, a scattering of the remaining herbs and either some totopos or slices of buttered granary bread on the side.

Feeds 6 as a starter
Time: 30 minutes + 1–4 hours chilling

200g scallops
200g sustainably caught king prawns
juice of 4 limes (about 200ml)
1–2 green chillies, roughly chopped
1 teaspoon fish sauce
1 teaspoon flaky sea salt
2½ tablespoons demerara sugar
1 small cucumber or ½ a large one
2 tablespoons reposado tequila
1 large banana shallot or 4 baby ones, finely sliced
about 12 cherry tomatoes, quartered
handful of chervil, coriander or mint (or a combination of all 3)
1 Hass avocado, diced
Totopos (page 50) or granary bread, to serve

Sopa seca

This gently spicy noodle dish is traditionally enjoyed as a first course after the requisite antojitos (nibbles), but I think it makes a wonderful family dish in the evening. Sopa seca means 'dry soup' and is so named because the broth is reduced to a thick and unctuous sauce that coats the soft, silky noodles. Both luxurious and comforting, it will keep you coming back for more, I guarantee it!

Heat the oil in a heavy-bottomed pan and, when it is warm but not hot, add the shallots, garlic and chilli. Season well with salt and pepper and sweat over a low to medium heat for about 10 minutes, until soft and translucent. Cover the fresh tomatoes with boiling water, leave for 30 seconds, then drain, skin and roughly chop. Add these or the tinned tomatoes to the shallots with the allspice, herbs and brown sugar, then simmer for 20 minutes to concentrate the flavours.

Meanwhile, heat the sunflower oil in a large frying pan or wok until it is shimmering hot. Sit the vermicelli in the oil in a single layer and fry for a few minutes, turning once or twice until it turns a rich golden colour. Remove with a slotted spoon and transfer to a large plate lined with kitchen paper.

Add the stock and capers to the tomato sauce and briefly blitz with a stick blender. Simmer for another 5 minutes before adding the vermicelli. Heat gently until the noodles have melted into the sauce and the liquid is absorbed, turning if necessary to coat them.

Feeds 4–5
Time: 45 minutes

50ml olive oil
2 baby shallots, finely chopped
1 garlic clove
1 green chilli, finely chopped (leave the seeds out if don't want it too hot)
sea salt and freshly ground black pepper
4 large, very ripe plum tomatoes or 1 x 400g tin chopped plum tomatoes
good pinch of allspice
few sprigs of fresh thyme
1 bay leaf
good pinch of brown sugar
sunflower oil, for deep-frying
225g vermicelli or angel hair pasta
400ml chicken or vegetable stock
2 tablespoons baby capers

For the sweet smoky salsa:
2 garlic cloves
50g Chipotles en adobo (page 238, optional)
2 tablespoons demerara sugar
juice and zest of 1 lime
½ teaspoon fish sauce

To serve:
1 x 150ml tub sour cream
handful of coriander, chopped
freshly grated pecorino cheese

To make the salsa, use a pestle and mortar to bash the garlic into a paste with the chipotles and sugar. Add the lime and fish sauce, season with plenty of black pepper and a little sea salt, then taste. The salsa should be spicy, sweet, salty, fresh and zesty.

Serve the noodles with a dollop of sour cream and a spoonful of the salsa, then sprinkle with the coriander and some pecorino.

NOTE: You can make this recipe in advance up to the point where the noodles and tomato sauce are cooked but not combined. Set them aside to cool until you are ready to eat, then add the noodles to the sauce, heat for about 5 minutes and serve.

Sea bass ceviche

I first tried ceviche (ce-vee-chay) on a beach on the Pacific coast of Mexico. I was immediately captivated by the fresh, fiery flavour of lime juice and chilli, and the delicate texture of the fish. In ceviche the lime juice 'cooks' the raw fish, resulting in a beautifully light dish that is very little work to prepare but has a whole lot of taste. Mexican vanilla softens the sometimes sharp flavour of the lime..

Spread the fish fillets in a single layer on a plate and put in the freezer for about 45 minutes. Slice the fish wafer thin and arrange on a wide, shallow serving dish. Mix the vanilla essence with the citrus juices and pour over the fish. Sprinkle on half the chilli and the onion, seasoning well with salt and pepper, and leave to marinate for 1 hour in the fridge.

When you are ready to eat, pour about half the marinade off the fish, drizzle with the olive oil and balsamic vinegar and scatter on the rest of the chilli, the radishes and the chopped coriander. Serve with salted crackers, freshly made totopos or simply fresh bread to mop up all the fiery juices.

Feeds 4
Time: 15 minutes + 2 hours freezing and marinating

300g fresh, line-caught sea bass, filleted and skinned (about 4 small fillets)
2 drops of vanilla essence
juice of 3 limes
juice of ½ a grapefruit
1–2 jalapeño or Thai green chillies, finely chopped
½ red onion, finely sliced
sea salt and freshly ground black pepper
2 tablespoons olive oil
about ½ tablespoon balsamic vinegar, or to taste
pinch of salt
4–5 radishes, finely sliced
large handful of coriander, chopped
salted crackers or Totopos (page 50) or bread, to serve

Octopus ceviche

It's best to buy frozen octopus for this dish rather than fresh, as the freezing helps to tenderise the flesh, leaving you with melt-in-the-mouth meat. Although it is called ceviche, in this case the octopus is actually cooked before you add the marinade.

Defrost the octopus thoroughly and cover with cold water. Add the onion, peppercorns and bay leaves. Bring to the boil and immediately turn the heat right down. Simmer extremely gently for 60–90 minutes, or until tender. Allow to cool in the cooking liquid.

Meanwhile, make the alioli by putting the garlic, egg yolks, lime juice and vinegar into a food processor or blender and blitzing until smooth. Put the oils into a jug and, with the processor motor running, pour them very slowly into the egg mixture until it emulsifies, then stepping up the pace to a steady, thin stream. Taste, season with salt and pepper and, if necessary, thin down with a few tablespoons of water so that you have a mayonnaise the consistency of pouring cream. Set aside.

Cut a small cross in the bottom of the tomatoes, put them in a heatproof bowl, then cover with boiling water and leave for 20–30 seconds. Peel off the skin, giving it a quick squeeze so as not to waste any of the juice. Roughly chop the flesh.

Cut the octopus into small, bite-sized pieces, discarding the head. Place in a bowl with the lime juice, tomatoes, olives, capers, chilli, shallots and marjoram. Season to taste.

Arrange on a shallow plate, drizzle with the alioli and serve with crispy totopos or tostadas. Let everyone dig in.

Feeds 6–8
Time: 2 hours

1 small frozen octopus
    (about 1.5kg)
1 onion, sliced
1 teaspoon peppercorns
4 bay leaves
4 large, ripe tomatoes
juice of 1–2 limes
10 fat, soft black olives
    (preferably Kalamata),
    stoned and chopped
2 tablespoons capers
1 fresh green chilli, very finely
    sliced
2 baby shallots, finely chopped
small handful of marjoram or
    thyme

For the alioli:
2 fat garlic cloves
2 egg yolks
juice of ½ a lime
1 tablespoon red wine vinegar
200ml sunflower oil
175ml extra virgin olive oil
sea salt and (preferably) white
    pepper
Totopos (page 50) or tostados
    (see page 54, step 1), to serve

El Pulpo

Salmon and avocado ceviche

This spicy ceviche recipe looks very pretty on the plate and is so simple to throw together. Two of its ingredients, soy sauce and sesame oil, are used all over Mexico City, which has much culinary influence from the Orient. The flavours go beautifully with raw fish, creamy avocado and hot fresh chillies. I also love using wild sea trout or very fresh mackerel in this recipe because they are often less expensive and more environmentally friendly than wild or organically farmed salmon.

Preheat the oven to 200°C/390°F/gas 6.

Skin the salmon fillets, then slice very thinly across the grain. Lay the pieces out neatly on each plate and squeeze over half the lime juice. Season with salt and pepper and put in the fridge for 10 minutes.

Brush the corn tortillas with olive oil and bake in the oven for about 5 minutes or until crisp and golden. Watch out – they are very easy to burn!

When you are ready to eat, cut the avocado into quarters, peel away the skin, remove the stone and cut the flesh into thin slices. Arrange in a fan on top of the salmon and scatter with the spring onions and chilli. Sprinkle over the rest of the lime juice, the soy sauce, the sesame oil and a drizzle of extra virgin olive oil and scatter over the coriander. Eat at once with the crisp tortillas.

Feeds 4
Time: 25 minutes

300g MSC-certified wild salmon or organic farmed salmon fillets
juice of 1 lime
sea salt and freshly ground black pepper
corn tortillas or pitta breads
extra virgin olive oil
1 avocado
2 spring onions, finely chopped
1–2 small, hot green chillies, finely sliced
1–2 teaspoons soy sauce
1 teaspoon sesame oil
large bunch of coriander, chopped

Fettuccine with chilli guajillo

Pasta dishes are hugely popular in Mexico City. This is an exotic but fairly simple recipe using one of Mexico's favourite chillies, the guajillo (gwah-hee-yoh), a mild chilli that gives food a spectacular, deep red colour. I love the rich earthiness of this dish.

Wipe the chillies with a clean, damp cloth and tear out the stems and seeds. Blitz in a food processor until they resemble tiny dice. Cover with boiling water and leave to soak for about 10 minutes, until they feel fairly soft to the bite. Drain, reserving the soaking liquid. Next, bash the garlic cloves with a rolling pin or pestle and slip off the skin. Chop or pulse the garlic into fine dice.

Heat the butter, olive oil and a good teaspoon of sea salt in a large saucepan over a medium heat. Be careful not to overheat the oil or you will lose all its flavour. When it is warm, add the garlic and cook gently for about 5 minutes (the oil should just be breaking a few bubbles on the surface). Add the chillies and continue to cook until the garlic is soft and golden, another 3–5 minutes. Turn off the heat and season with more salt to taste and plenty of pepper.

When you are ready to eat, bring a large saucepan of water to a brisk boil, add the reserved chilli water and season with a teaspoon of fine sea salt. Add the pasta and cook until al dente – soft but still with a bit of bite (about 8 minutes). Drain the pasta, reserving a cup of the cooking water.

To serve, gently toss the pasta in the chilli oil. Scatter with the coriander and serve with plenty of grated Parmesan and wedges of lime. This is lovely with a green salad.

Feeds 6
Time: 45 minutes

15 guajillo chillies
3 heads of garlic, cloves
   separated
50g butter
280ml extra virgin olive oil
sea salt and freshly ground
   black pepper
700g fettuccine pasta
large handful of fresh
   coriander, roughly chopped

To serve:
200g Parmesan or Gran Padano
   cheese, grated
2 limes, cut into wedges

Spaghetti with ricotta and courgette flowers

When I first cooked this recipe I used wonderfully peppery nasturtium flowers from my garden because the courgette season was over. If you can't get hold of the flowers, toss rocket or shredded mustard leaf through the pasta at the last minute and it will still taste great.

Toast the almonds in a dry frying pan or warm oven (140°C/275°F/Gas 1) until they are pale golden, then set aside. Roughly chop when they have cooled a little.

Heat a large frying pan over a medium heat and add half the olive oil. Add the onion and turn the heat down a little so it sweats slowly in the oil. After a few minutes, add the garlic and half the chilli and season generously with salt and pepper. If the chilli is mild, you can add the rest later on if you wish.

When the onions and garlic have sweated for about 10 minutes, add the courgettes and another tablespoon of olive oil to the pan. Season again if necessary. Cover the pan with a lid and cook over a low heat for 5 minutes before adding the wine, lime zest and juice. Cook with the lid on for about 15–20 minutes, stirring from time to time, until the courgettes have collapsed into a silky soft heap. Meanwhile, cook the pasta in plenty of well-salted, boiling water until al dente.

Stir the ricotta, Parmesan, remaining 3 tablespoons of olive oil and all but a sprinkling of the herbs into the courgette mixture, then gently toss in the flowers, saving a few for garnish.

Drain the pasta and drizzle with a little extra olive oil. Toss with the courgette mixture and taste for seasoning. Serve sprinkled with the remaining herbs, reserved flowers, some extra Parmesan and the toasted almonds.

NOTE: This makes a delicious supper but also a very pretty starter.

Feeds 4
Time: 35 minutes

60g blanched almonds
120ml olive oil
1 medium onion, chopped
2 fat garlic cloves, finely chopped
1 green chilli, finely diced
sea salt and freshly ground black pepper
4 medium courgettes, roughly sliced
glass of dry, fruity white wine (a dryish chardonnay or burgundy works well)
zest and juice of 1 lime
300g fusilli pasta
150g ricotta cheese
1 heaped tablespoon grated Parmesan or Gran Padano cheese
handful each of chervil and basil, finely chopped
handful of courgette flowers, nasturtium flowers and leaves, or rocket leaves

flower power

The Mexicans have been eating flowers for centuries, whether courgette flowers, which grow abundantly through much of the country, nasturtiums, hibiscus, roses or countless other species. It is a place where every possible ingredient that can be eaten will be eaten, so it is totally normal for cooks to forage for edible plants and leaves to add to their recipes.

Hibiscus flowers are dried and boiled up to make thirst-quenching, cranberry-tasting Agua frescas (page 200); rose petals are added to sauces, turned into syrups and used to flavour ice creams and puddings; courgette flowers are sautéd and stuffed inside tacos and quesadillas, or filled and deep-fried. We love this approach, using whatever can be picked locally to decorate and flavour food.

Cooking and garnishing with flowers is great fun, but it is important to remember that not every flower, or even every part of it, is edible, so consult a good reference book before using them. Once you know it's safe to eat, discard the pistils and stamens, and wash and separate the petals from the rest of the flower just before use to keep everything looking fresh. Avoid flowers that have been sprayed with pesticides (including those bought from florists), and never harvest anything growing by the roadside.

Queso fundido with chorizo

Queso fundido is Mexican fondue, normally made with a melting string cheese from Oaxaca. At the restaurant we use a mixture of oozing mozzarella and a tasty mature Cheddar, which we bake until melted and then scoop into hot flour tortillas. The fondue can be made with just cheese, or have a variety of extras sitting on top or under the surface. This recipe is a favourite at Wahaca; the slow-cooked chorizo sauce goes amazingly with the gooey cheese.

Preheat the oven 180°C/350°F/gas 4.

With a knife, mark a cross on the bottom of each tomato, just piercing the skin. Cover with boiling water and count to 20. Drain, run under cold water, then peel and dice them into small cubes.

Heat a heavy-bottomed saucepan over a medium heat and add the oil and chorizo. Cook for 5 minutes, letting the chorizo release its fat and breaking up the pieces with a wooden spoon. Add the onion, celery, garlic and cumin and cook for about 10 minutes, until the onion is soft and translucent. Season with salt and pepper, add the tequila, tomatoes and purée and cook until most of the moisture has evaporated and you are left with a ragu-like chorizo sauce. Finally, add the oregano and check for seasoning.

Spread the mixture in the bottom of a gratin dish. Mix the 2 cheeses together in a bowl, then sprinkle over the chorizo mixture. Place in the oven for 10 minutes or until the cheese has melted. You could also put the gratin dish under the grill if you prefer. Serve with warm tortillas.

Feeds 6 as a starter
Time: 30 minutes

3 large plum tomatoes
½ tablespoon olive oil
165g chorizo, skinned and roughly chopped
1 small Spanish onion, finely diced
2 sticks of celery, finely chopped
2 garlic cloves, crushed
½ teaspoon ground cumin
sea salt and freshly ground black pepper
3 tablespoons tequila
1 teaspoon tomato purée
2 teaspoons roughly chopped oregano
125g mozzarella cheese, grated
75g Cheddar cheese, grated
warm flour tortillas, to serve

Queso fundido with mushroom al ajillo

A Mexican cheese fondue baked with chilli-spiked, buttery mushrooms and hot flour tortillas. This is my kind of supper dish for autumnal comfort eating.

Preheat the oven to 180°C/350°F/gas 4.

With a knife, mark a cross on the bottom of each tomato, just piercing the skin. Cover with boiling water and count to 20. Drain, run under cold water, then peel, de-seed and roughly chop them.

Heat a medium-sized frying pan over a high heat and, when it is smoking hot, add half the butter. Stir in the mushrooms, season well with salt and pepper and cook for 10 minutes. By this time, the mushrooms will have released their liquid, most of which will have reduced.

Set aside the mushrooms, put the pan back over a medium heat, adding the remaining butter along with the onion, garlic, half the chile de árbol and the thyme leaves. Cook over a medium-low heat until the onion begins to soften and lightly brown, about 10 minutes. Return the mushrooms to the pan along with the tomatoes and the ale and simmer until most of the moisture has evaporated. Finally, add the parsley, taste and season if necessary. If you want more chilli, you can add it at this stage.

Spread the mushroom mixture, which should look like a thick ragu, in the bottom of a gratin dish. Mix the 2 cheeses together in a small bowl, then sprinkle them on top of the mixture. Heat in the oven for about 10 minutes or until the cheese has melted all over the mushrooms. Alternatively, place the dish under a hot grill.

Serve immediately with hot flour tortillas.

Feeds 6 as a light starter
Time: 30 minutes

3 large tomatoes
2 tablespoons butter
4 large Portobello mushrooms, or about 300g mixed wild mushrooms, chopped into bite-sized pieces
sea salt and freshly ground black pepper
1 small Spanish onion, finely chopped
2 garlic cloves, crushed
1 chile de árbol, finely chopped
leaves from a small handful of thyme sprigs
3 tablespoons dark ale
small handful of flat leaf parsley, roughly chopped
125g mozzarella cheese, grated
75g Cheddar cheese, grated
hot flour tortillas, to serve

Chilorio

Chilorio (Mexican pulled pork cooked in a rich, intensely flavoured sauce) is one of the specialities I love most from the north of Mexico. It is traditionally served as a starter, with plenty of hot flour tortillas to hand round and salsa on the side. It is also utterly delicious on top of the Queso fundido opposite or, for a more English take, served with mashed potatoes and greens, or stuffed inside a jacket potato. This recipe is adapted from one by Diana Kennedy, and I like to cook it with neck end of pork, which is both cheap and beautifully marbled with fat, giving the final dish bags of good, meaty taste.

Cut the meat into rough pieces about 5cm square. Place in a heavy-bottomed pan, barely cover with water and season generously with salt. Bring to the boil, uncovered. Lower the heat so that the water simmers without boiling too vigorously, and cook until the water has evaporated, about 90 minutes. By this time, the meat should be soft and falling apart. Chop or shred it into fine pieces, leaving the fat in the pan.

Meanwhile, stem and de-seed the chillies and cover them with boiling water. Soak for 10 minutes, then drain. Put the vinegar and cold water into a blender with the garlic, cumin and oregano and whiz to get a smooth liquid. Add the chillies in 2 batches and whiz to a thick purée. Add a tiny bit more water if the paste is too thick, to help the blades go round.

Put the saucepan back on the heat and add half the lard. When the fat has melted, add the chilli purée and cook, stirring, for a few minutes. Add the rest of the lard, return the shredded meat to the pan and cook over a low heat for 15–20 minutes, until the mixture is quite dry. Serve at once.

NOTE: Why not make a batch of the sauce and store it for future use? It will keep for several months in an airtight container in the fridge.

Feeds 6–8
Time: 2 hours

900g neck end of pork, boned
sea salt and freshly ground
  black pepper
8 ancho chillies
90ml good-quality cider
  vinegar
175ml cold water
8 garlic cloves
¼ teaspoon ground cumin
leaves from a small bunch of
  oregano or thyme
50g lard

AUTUMN STEW

POWER TO THE PIBIL

platos

"BIGGER PLATES"

When we opened Wahaca, our dream was to serve the kind of street food that you can find in the markets and streets of Mexico – small delicious plates that you share with friends, enabling you to try as many different tastes as possible. At the same time, we instinctively wanted to offer some bigger dishes, the incredibly good cantina 'platos fuertes', so that if you happened to be in the mood for a great plate of food all to yourself, there was that option, no sharing allowed.

NO SHARING ALLOWED!

BAKED SEA BREAM

fuertes

In traditional Mexican cooking, the ratio of meat to sauce is about one to three, so you tend to get a small chunk of meat sitting in a pool of rich sauce seasoned with chillies and spices and enriched with ground nuts, pumpkin or sesame seeds, and sometimes dried fruit. This makes the cuisine more economical and certainly greener than European cooking, where we are accustomed to great slabs of meat with very little sauce. These complex sauces are called moles (moh-lays), and they are as varied as Mexico's ingredients, with different versions cooked up and down the country, depending on the state you're in and the person doing the cooking.

On our first staff trip to Mexico we took twelve of the team to Oaxaca to visit a

cooperative of farmers that produces a mezcal we serve at the bar. The farmers were poor but fed us superbly. I still remember that delicious lunch, served in rustic bowls, as if it were yesterday: a tiny morsel of poached chicken (they had killed two of their own for us that morning) floating in a rich, mouth-watering yellow mole (page 126), typical of the region.

We scooped up the sauce with large, freshly baked corn tortillas that we rolled up like cigars. By the end of lunch, moved by the overwhelming generosity of the family (and perhaps also by their pretty amazing mezcal), half of us were in tears. None of us will ever forget that meal.

Baked sea bream a la Veracruzana

This is a beautifully simple recipe that you can put together at the weekend for friends or family, and tastes so good that it will be long remembered. In fact it has now become a staple recipe when I am entertaining: the smoky mezcal, sweet tomatoes and light spice of the jalapeños make a really spectacular marriage of flavours. If you can't get hold of sea bream, use any white-fleshed fish.

Preheat the oven to 200°C/390°F/gas 6.

Wash the sea bream inside and out and pat dry. Fold a large piece of foil in half to make a generous, double-layered wrapping for the fish inside a baking tray. Lay the bream on top, stuff with the thyme and season generously, inside and out, with salt and pepper. Dot with the butter, pour over the white wine and 50ml of the mezcal, then wrap up the fish, tightly sealing the edges of the foil. Bake for 25–35 minutes, or until the fish is just cooked.

Meanwhile, heat a large frying pan over a medium heat and add the oil and onions. Turn the heat down a touch and sweat the onions until they turn soft and translucent, about 10 minutes. Add the garlic, bay leaves, allspice, marjoram, capers and chillies, season with plenty of salt and pepper and cook for a further 10–15 minutes, by which time the onions will taste incredibly sweet. Add the tomatoes, simmer for another 10 minutes and season to taste.

Once the fish is cooked, pour its juices into the tomato sauce and stir to combine. Serve chunks of the fish with spoonfuls of the sauce. This is delicious with very simply cooked long-grain rice.

Feeds 4–6
Time: 50 minutes

1 or more sea bream (1.4kg in total), gutted and de-scaled
sprigs of thyme
sea salt and freshly ground black pepper
50g butter
150ml dry white wine
150ml mezcal, or reposado tequila
4 tablespoons extra virgin olive oil
2 onions, finely chopped
4 garlic cloves, sliced
2–3 bay leaves
½ teaspoon ground allspice
sprigs of marjoram, roughly chopped
2 tablespoons small capers
50g pickled jalapeño chillies
2 x 400g tins plum tomatoes

Grilled sea bass
a la pimienta

Pimienta means 'pepper', and here we use lots of it to add great character and punch to a sauce of silky, sweet onions. This recipe works well with any type of flat white fish. At Wahaca we are very aware of issues surrounding over-fishing, so we favour lesser-used species, such as grey mullet, over the likes of swordfish and tuna. This is such a favourite on the menu that we rarely take it off; it is a cinch to make and utterly delicious

In a dry, fairly hot frying pan, toast the pumpkin seeds for a few minutes, until golden and just starting to pop. When they are cool, roughly chop.

Meanwhile, gently heat the olive oil in a heavy-bottomed pan and sweat the onion, garlic and chilli for 20–25 minutes, stirring occasionally, until the onions are soft, golden and translucent and beginning to sweeten.

Stir the pumpkin seeds into the onions and season with salt and masses of freshly ground black pepper. The pepper is the main seasoning for this dish; the sauce wants to have a real edge to it to balance the sweetness of the onions. Add the lime juice and water and simmer for 5 minutes, or until the onions are swimming in a golden syrup.

Heat a frying pan until it is smoking hot. Add a knob of butter and, when it is sizzling, fry the fish skin side down until the flesh just starts to turn opaque. Turn and fry on the other side for a minute or so, depending on the thickness of the fish. Divide the fillets between serving plates and top with spoonfuls of the golden, spicy onions, chopped coriander and wedges of lime. This is beautiful with a side salad dressed with Black bean and sweetcorn salsa (page 230).

Feeds 6
Time: 40 minutes

125g pumpkin seeds
120ml extra virgin olive oil
1kg onions, finely sliced
8 fat garlic cloves, finely
  chopped
2–3 fresh green chillies, finely
  chopped
sea salt and masses of freshly
  ground black pepper
juice of 3 limes
100 ml water
knob of butter
1kg line-caught sea bass fillets
small bunch of coriander,
  roughly chopped
lime wedges, to serve

Grilled salmon in sweet, smoky tamarind sauce

The Mexicans are mad about tamarind. They eat it with seafood, with meat and, more bizarrely, coated in chilli sugar as an insanely addictive sweet. The combination of the refreshingly sour tamarind and smoky chipotle is one of those happy food matches that just sings.

A couple of hours before you wish to eat, mix all the marinade ingredients together. Place the salmon in a small, shallow dish and pour over the marinade. Cover and chill for 2 hours, turning once halfway through.

When you're ready to start cooking, preheat the grill. Place a large frying pan on the hob and heat until it is smoking hot, then add a drizzle of groundnut oil. When it is hot, add the salmon slices, skin side down, and fry for 5–6 minutes. Put the pan under the grill, keeping the handle clear of the heat source, and cook for a further 3–4 minutes. Remove the fish and wrap in foil.

Meanwhile, pour the marinade through a sieve into a small pan, bring to a gentle boil and reduce until it becomes thick and syrupy. Serve the fish with greens and rice, covered with the hot sauce. It's also delicious with either the Gooseberry and avocado salsa or a Salsa verde (pages 224 and 226).

NOTE: The tamarind sauce is also a delicious marinade for ribs.

Feeds 6
Time: 25 minutes + 2 hours marinating

1kg wild salmon, gutted, descaled and cut into 6 slices

For the marinade:
4 tablespoons tamarind purée
2 tablespoons Japanese soy sauce
3 tablespoons groundnut or sunflower oil
juice of 2 large limes
4 tablespoons demerara sugar
3cm fresh ginger, peeled and grated
2 garlic cloves, bashed
2 dried chipotle chillies, soaked in hot water and pounded to a paste
handful of mint leaves, roughly chopped
handful of coriander leaves and root, roughly chopped
sea salt and freshly ground black pepper

¡Holy mole!

Mole ('moh-lay') is the Mexican word for sauce – when we talk about cooking a mole and storing it in the freezer, we are never referring to small furry creatures. Hence 'guacamole', meaning avocado sauce (possibly our favourite type of mole at Wahaca).

In Mexico moles range from simple to complex, with the mole negro Oaxaqueño being one of the most intricate versions; it uses four or five types of dried chilli, five types of nut, dried fruit, plantain, herbs and spices, and the last time I made it, it took me a whole weekend, even with three helpers stirring and grinding! By comparison, the Amarillo (page 126) is a relatively simple dish, using a few dried chillies, no nuts and no fruit.

Moles are as intrinsic to Mexican cookery as gravy is to the British, so every cook in the country will have her own special recipe handed down through the generations from grandmother to daughter. They are made for special occasions, such as weddings, birthday parties and the Day of the Dead (what we know as the feast of All Souls, 2 November), not least because of the time and effort it takes to amass all the ingredients and then toast, fry, grind and cook them. I think families would probably be prouder of making the best mole in the village than earning the most money; there are even local and national mole competitions throughout the year.

The state of Oaxaca is famous for having seven moles to its name, so it is fitting that we, who take our name from this most culinary of states, love mole so much. At work we are currently serving a black mole made in Guanajuato by a cooperative of single mothers. We think it is delicious, but we constantly have plans to make more.

Chicken with peanut mole

This is a modern take on a traditional mole recipe, using only one type of nut instead of five, and far fewer chillies. It is the type of recipe that a Mexican might make at home for an everyday supper, rather than the more complex recipes that are cooked for feasts and celebrations.

Preheat the oven to 180°C/350°F/gas 4.

Place the chicken in a large saucepan with the onion, bay leaves and peppercorns and cover with water. If you also have carrot or stick of celery in the fridge, roughly chop and add to the water as they will give lots of flavour. Put over a medium heat, cover and bring to boiling point. Turn the heat right down so that the water is just simmering, occasionally breaking bubbles on the surface. Simmer for 20–25 minutes, then turn the heat off and leave to cool in the poaching liquid (which is now your lovely stock).

Meanwhile, heat a large frying pan and dry-roast the onion wedges, tomatoes and garlic, turning every now and then until they are blackened, blistered and soft. Place them all in a blender, remembering to slip off the garlic skin.

Feeds 6
Time: 1 hour

1 large free-range chicken
   (about 2kg)
1 small onion, cut in half
2 bay leaves
10 peppercorns

For the mole:
1 small onion, cut into 6
   wedges
2 large ripe tomatoes
6 garlic cloves, unpeeled
6 allspice berries
1 cinnamon stick
4 chipotle chillies
2 ancho chillies
175g unsalted peanuts
45g lard or 3 tablespoons
   olive oil
50g raisins
sea salt and freshly ground
   black pepper

To serve:
freshly chopped coriander
1 red onion, finely chopped
sour cream or crème fraîche

Lightly toast the allspice and cinnamon in a dry frying pan for about 20 seconds, then grind to a fine powder and add them to the blender. Prepare the ancho and chipotle chillies as on page 86, discarding the seeds. Set aside half the chipotles and put the rest of the chillies in the blender.

Fry the peanuts in a tablespoon of lard until they are lightly browned all over, then set aside. Fry the raisins in the same fat until they are caramelised (a few minutes). Add the peanuts and raisins to the blender and whiz everything together, adding just enough stock from the poached chicken to loosen the blades between pulses. You want a thick, smooth paste. Season to taste with salt and pepper, and add more chipotle if you like it more fiery and smoky.

Heat the remaining lard in a deep pan and, when it is hot, add the sauce, stirring constantly for 2–3 minutes so that it does not burn. Turn the heat down after a minute, being careful as the mixture will spit. Stir in enough chicken stock to loosen the sauce to the consistency of double cream, about 400–700ml. Season to taste.

Joint the chicken, remove the skin and either shred the flesh into the sauce or serve whole chicken bits with spoonfuls of the peanut mole over it, garnished with the coriander, red onion and sour cream.

Mole amarillo

We first tried this yellow mole outside Oaxaca's 20 de Noviembre market, where it was mixed with shredded chicken plus a little corn dough and stuffed inside tortillas, baked into empanadas and served with the outrageously hot chile de agua and onion relish. We tried it again a few days later at the house of one of our mezcal suppliers; his wife cooked it outside over an open fire and fed fourteen of us; it was so good that some actually wept! It is not a complicated sauce to make, although I have substituted the chillies they use in Oaxaca for ones more readily available in Britain. I dream about putting this on the Wahaca menu. It is such a wonderfully rich, homely-tasting stew.

Fill a large pan with water and add the onion, garlic and bay leaves, season with salt and bring to simmering point. Simmer gently for 10 minutes before adding the pork pieces. Simmer very gently for a further 15 minutes before adding the chicken pieces. Cook for 15 minutes before turning off the heat and leaving to cool.

To make the mole, toast and rehydrate the chillies, as on page 86, soaking them for 20 minutes. Now toast all the spices in the dry frying pan until they smell fragrant, about 5–10 minutes. Grind to a powder, then transfer to a blender. Add the onion, tomatoes and garlic to the pan and dry-roast, as on page 234. Transfer to the blender as they cook, remembering to slip off the garlic skins. Drain the chillies and add them to the blender with the drained tomatillos and oregano and whiz for 5 minutes to a smooth purée.

Heat the lard in a pan and, when very hot, add the purée, stirring all the time to prevent it spitting. Turn the heat down and cook, stirring occasionally, for 10 minutes. Thin the masa harina with just enough of the chicken stock to make a smooth paste, then add to the mole. Stir in 2 cups of the stock, add the tarragon and cook for 15 minutes over a low heat. Taste and adjust the seasoning if necessary…

Feeds at least 10, but freezes beautifully
Time: about 90 minutes

1 onion
2–3 garlic cloves
2–3 bay leaves
sea salt
450g neck of pork, cut into 2–3cm dice
1 large chicken, jointed into 8 pieces
450g new potatoes, cut into chunks
1 large acorn or butternut squash, peeled and cut into chunks
450g green beans, cut in half
1 cauliflower, broken into florets
hot tortillas or steamed rice, to serve

For the mole:
6 guajillo chillies
2 ancho chillies
1 teaspoon black peppercorns
8 cloves
10 allspice berries
1 teaspoon cumin seeds
1 large onion, quartered
2 large tomatoes
5 garlic cloves, unpeeled
1 x 790g tin tomatillos, drained
small bunch of fresh oregano or 1 teaspoon dried oregano, preferably Mexican
40g lard
2 tablespoons masa harina
small handful of tarragon, chopped

Meanwhile, cook the vegetables. Fill a pan with water, add a teaspoon of salt and bring to the boil. Add the potatoes and cook until tender. Remove with a slotted spoon, then add the squash and cook until just tender. Remove with the slotted spoon, then cook the beans and cauliflower in the same way, removing each when they still have a slight bite. Do not overcook or they will turn to a mush in the stew.

Drain the meat and add to the mole. Heat through, adding more stock if necessary. About 5 minutes before serving, add all the vegetables to heat through. Serve the stew in shallow bowls making sure everyone gets a piece of chicken and pork and some of the vegetables swimming in spoonfuls of the mole. Serve with hot tortillas or, if you prefer, with rice.

NOTE: Traditionally a plant called hoja santa is used in this recipe. If you can get hold of it, finely shred 3 large leaves and add them in place of the tarragon.

Duck breast with a rich tomato, jalapeño and green olive sauce

This recipe is based on one from Zarela Martinez's amazing cookbook *Zarela's Veracruz*. I like to buy a whole duck, use the breasts and fat for this dish, and keep the legs for confit and the body for stock. It's great value, as well as being a treat, and you can freeze the pieces you don't want to cook immediately. Otherwise, just buy the duck breasts and serve with hot steamed rice and a happy grin. The combination of duck, tequila and spicy tomato sauce is guaranteed to please!

Season the duck breasts well with salt and pepper and leave in the fridge overnight or for at least 2 hours.

Preheat the oven to 200°C/390°F/gas 6. Heat the fat in a large pan, add the shallots and garlic and sweat over a medium heat until the shallots are soft. Add the tomatoes, herbs and chillies, season well with salt, pepper and a good pinch of brown sugar and cook for 20 minutes. Add the stock, olives, bay leaves and tequila, turn up the heat a little and reduce the sauce for a further 20 minutes or until it has thickened and turned glossy.

Brush the skin side of the duck with oil. Heat a non-stick frying pan over a high heat and, when it is smoking hot, cook the duck breasts skin side down for 4–5 minutes. Turn and cook for a further 4–5 minutes on the other side before transferring them to a roasting tin and finishing off in the oven for 5 minutes more. Meanwhile, add any fat from the frying pan to the tomato sauce.

Remove the duck and rest, covered in foil, for 8 minutes. This will allow the juices to run back into the meat and result in juicy pink breasts. When they are rested, thinly slice and add any cooking juices to the sauce. Serve the slivers of meat with some of the hot sauce poured over, accompanied by some simple steamed rice.

Feeds 4–5
Time: 3 hours + at least 2 hours chilling

2 medium duck breasts (approx. 240g each)
sea salt and freshly ground black pepper
2 tablespoons duck fat, lard or olive oil
5 small banana shallots or 2 large ones, sliced
6 garlic cloves, crushed
2 x 400g tins plum tomatoes
small bunch each of thyme and marjoram, roughly chopped
50g pickled jalapeño chillies, roughly chopped
good pinch of brown sugar
250–300ml chicken or duck stock
100g green olives, stoned and roughly chopped
2–3 bay leaves
100ml reposado tequila

Pork belly carnitas

Carnitas is one of the most mouth-watering dishes in the Mexican repertoire: succulent chunks of pork that are slowly braised in their own fat, just like duck confit. This is glorious served with vivid green Gooseberry and avocado salsa, or Robust salsa verde if you can get the tomatillos.

Preheat the oven to 130°C/250°F/gas 1.

Cut the pork belly into 6 roughly equal pieces. Rub with salt and leave to sit for 1 hour.

Put the pork chunks into a large casserole pan with the rest of the ingredients and bring to simmering point. Cover well with a tight-fitting lid or foil and cook in the oven for 2–3 hours until the pork is so soft that it can be cut with a spoon.

Scoop out the pieces with a slotted spoon and arrange them on a baking sheet. Turn the oven up to 190°C/375°F/gas 5. Roast the pork for about 30 minutes, until the pieces are crispy, golden and caramelised.

Roughly chop the meat and serve on a wooden board or heated plate with bowls of coriander, white onion or shallot, wedges of lime, a salsa and warm tortillas for making your own tacos.

Feeds 6–8
Time: 3½ hours + 1 hour resting

1 pork belly, boned
500g lard
2 bay leaves
5 garlic cloves, bashed
2 oranges, sliced
1 teaspoon peppercorns
500ml cola drink
handful of thyme sprigs
sea salt

To serve:
handful of fresh coriander, chopped
1 white onion or a few shallots, chopped
lime wedges
Gooseberry and avocado salsa (page 227) or Robust salsa verde (page 226)
warm corn tortillas

Tinga de pollo

This street-food classic can be found on virtually every street corner in Mexico, and it's been on the menu at Wahaca since the day we opened, only sometimes being replaced with a mole in the winter. It is easy to prepare and tastes extremely good – the slow-cooked onions adding sweetness to the fire of the chipotles. The sauce is also delicious with slow-cooked pork (page 134).

Place the chicken in a large pot with the onion, garlic and peppercorns and cover with water. If you have a carrot or stick of celery in the fridge, roughly chop them and add to the water as they will give lots of flavour. Put the pan over a medium heat, cover and bring to boiling point. Turn the heat right down so that the water is just simmering, occasionally breaking bubbles on the surface. Simmer for about 20 minutes, then turn the heat off and leave to cool in the poaching liquid. Shred the meat with 2 forks, reserving the lovely stock.

Soak the chipotles in boiling water for 10 minutes. Meanwhile, heat a large frying pan over a medium heat and dry-roast the fresh tomatoes (is using) and garlic cloves, as on page 222. When the skin of the tomatoes is blackened and blistered, put in a blender, along with the garlic (remember to slip off the skin), the herbs and chipotles. Whiz to a purée and season well with salt and pepper.

Heat the lard in a large pan and add the onions. Sauté until translucent, then turn the heat right down and cook for 10 minutes to release the sugars. Add the blended sauce, the sugar and stock, bring to the boil and check for seasoning. Simmer for 10 minutes over a medium-high heat.

Finally, add the shredded chicken, turn the heat down and cook for 15–20 minutes, until all the flavours have melded together. Serve with a bowl of steaming hot rice and tortillas (to make tacos), with guacamole or a fresh salsa and wedges of lime.

Feeds 6
Time: 1 hour

1 medium free-range chicken (about 1.5kg)
1 large onion, quartered
6 garlic cloves, bashed
10 peppercorns

For the tinga sauce:
4–5 chipotles, stemmed and de-seeded
6 large, ripe tomatoes or 2 x 400g tins plum tomatoes
6 garlic cloves, unpeeled
small handful of fresh oregano leaves or 1 teaspoon dried oregano
2 bay leaves
sea salt and freshly ground black pepper
2 tablespoons lard or olive oil
2 medium onions, sliced
1–2 tablespoons dark brown sugar or palm sugar
85ml chicken stock

To serve:
steamed rice
warm tortillas
Guacamole (page 194) or salsa of your choice
lime wedges

Pork pibil

This is our bestselling dish at Wahaca and one of my favourite recipes from Mexico. It comes from the Yucatán and uses two local products: achiote, a spicy paste made from the ground red berries of the annatto tree, which turns the marinade brick red; and the habañero chilli, which gives it a lovely touch of fire. You can buy achiote online or from specialist shops. If you prefer your food not too hot, simply leave the chilli out. We use neck end of pork, which is marbled with delicious fat that melts into the sauce. For the tastiest, most tender pork, marinate it the day before cooking.

First make the marinade. Warm the spices in a dry frying pan for a few minutes, then grind to a fine powder. Place in a blender with the achiote, vinegar, onion, garlic, herbs, salt and olive oil and pulse to start breaking up the achiote. Slowly pour in the orange juice with the motor running to get a smooth paste.

Pour about two-thirds of the marinade over the pork, ensuring that it is thoroughly coated. Refrigerate overnight. Freeze your remaining marinade or keep it fresh for a week in the fridge (and try it with something else, like barbecued chicken).

Preheat the oven to 130°C/250°F/gas 1.

Transfer the pork and its marinade to a large casserole dish and add the chopped chilli and butter. Bring to simmering point, cover with foil and a tight-fitting lid and cook as slowly as possible for 3–4 hours, until the pork is soft and falling apart.

Serve chunks of pork in deep bowls with rice or steamed potatoes, lots of sauce and piles of the Pink pickled onions on top.

Feeds 10–12, but freezes well
Time: 3½–4 hours + overnight marinating

3kg neck of pork, cut into a few large pieces
1 habañero or Scotch bonnet chilli, de-seeded and finely chopped
50g butter

For the marinade:
1 teaspoon allspice berries
2 teaspoons freshly ground cumin seeds
½ teaspoon cloves
1 teaspoon peppercorns
100g achiote paste
3 tablespoons cider vinegar
1 medium onion, coarsely chopped
3 fat garlic cloves, coarsely chopped
large bunch of fresh oregano or 1 teaspoon dried oregano
3 fresh bay leaves
2 tablespoons sea salt
3 tablespoons olive oil
juice of 6 oranges (about 450ml)

To serve:
steamed rice or potatoes
Pink pickled onions (page 231)

Edson and Renan's pozole

With so much talent in the kitchens at Wahaca, I asked our head chefs to come to a cooking day at my house armed with a favourite recipe to recreate. Edson and Renan chose this classic, found in markets throughout Mexico. As with most slow-cooked pork dishes, they used the neck cut, which has great marbling to it, resulting in tender, succulent pieces of meat – essential for a proper pozole. Served with bowls of fresh lime, finely sliced cabbage and radish, the brothy mix of hominy (large white corn kernels), the falling-apart pork and the hot salsa make a fresh-tasting, deeply satisfying meal that will warm the cockles.

Soak the hominy in water overnight.

Put the pork in a large stockpot, cover with cold water, sprinkle with the salt and bring to the boil. Once the scum floats to the surface, skim it away and add an onion studded with the cloves, the peppercorns, bay leaves and 2 of the garlic cloves, bashed. Simmer gently for 1 hour, or until the pork is tender.

Meanwhile, drain the hominy and put it in a saucepan with enough chicken stock to cover. Bring to the boil and simmer gently for 1 hour or until tender.

Chop the second onion and the remaining garlic. Heat a frying pan over a high heat, then add the olive oil and onion. Cook over a medium heat for a few minutes before adding the chopped garlic, the chillies and spices. Season with salt and pepper and fry until soft and fragrant.

When the pork is tender and falling apart, add the hominy and cooked onion mixture. Simmer for another 10–15 minutes, then season to taste.

Serve with tortillas (if you wish), bowls of lime wedges, thinly sliced radishes, chopped tomatoes and shredded cabbage, and extra hot salsa for a dash of heat.

Feeds 8
Time: 90 minutes + overnight soaking

1 kg hominy (aka maize for pozole)
1kg pork neck or shoulder, diced in 5cm chunks
2 teaspoons sea salt
2 medium onions
3 cloves
5 whole peppercorns
2 bay leaves
4 garlic cloves
approx. 600ml chicken stock
1 tablespoon olive oil
2 green chillies, finely chopped
1 teaspoon freshly ground cumin seeds
½ teaspoon cayenne pepper
½ teaspoon chilli flakes
sea salt and freshly ground black pepper

To serve:
tortillas (optional)
lime wedges
radishes
tomatoes
cabbage
Extra hot chilli salsa (page 239)

Smoky, tender pork ribs

This recipe came out of the Wahaca 'butchery day' at my house. Having broken down the half pig that arrived at my door at 8 o'clock that morning, head chefs Edson, Elki, Leo, Edson, Steve and Renan fell upon the different cuts of meat with glee. It was brilliant to see everyone's minds whirring at the same time, and the results were as tasty as you might imagine. In Mexico, nose-to-tail cooking is de rigueur, with every single part of an animal being used in recipes. These ribs were the brainchild of Renan. They are smoky, sweet and sticky with a touch of spice.

Ask your butcher to remove any tough skin from the pork ribs and score them diagonally for you. Place them in a shallow baking dish. Dissolve the salt, sugar and Chipotles en adobo (if using) in a saucepan of warm water. IPour enough of the liquid over the ribs to cover, then marinate overnight, or for at least 2 hours. Discard the marinade.

To make the sauce, cook the onion and garlic in the olive oil over a low–medium heat until soft. Cool, season with a teaspoon of salt and add the remaining ingredients. Whiz in a blender until smooth and check the seasoning.

Preheat the oven to 200°C/390°F/gas 6. Place the ribs on a rack in a roasting tin filled with water, making sure the ribs don't touch the water. Cover with foil and place in the oven for about 2 hours, checking to see if tender after 90 minutes. When the ribs are soft, remove them from the oven and discarding the liquid from the tin. All of this can be done a day in advance if you like.

Light a barbecue or preheat the grill to its highest temperature. Baste the ribs with the chipotle sauce, place them on the barbecue or grill rack and cook for 10–15 minutes, until they are caramelised, blackened in places and smelling delicious.

These ribs are a great side dish for a barbecue, or serve them as a main course with rice and Chilli-spiked grilled corn (page 51).

Feeds 6–8
Time: about 2½ hours + at least 2 hours marinating

800g pork ribs
30g sea salt
40g soft brown sugar
2 teaspoons Chipotles en adobo (page 238, optional)

For the sauce:
1 small onion, diced
1 garlic clove, finely chopped
1 tablespoon olive oil
sea salt
2 teaspoons Chipotles en adobo (page 238)
2 teaspoons brown sugar
1 tablespoon reposado tequila

Autumn stew with pipián

In Mexico, pumpkin seeds have been used to add protein to dishes for centuries, and are sometimes ground into a sauce called a pipián, a type of mole. Here it gives a nuttiness that beautifully complements the sweetness of the squash and quince. If you can't get hold of quinces, leave them out or use apples instead. This is a really fine, satisfying vegetarian stew that is good with any kind of squash or pumpkin.

Preheat the oven to 200°C/390°F/gas 6.

Top and tail the squash, peel and cut into large, bite-sized chunks. Peel, core and dice the quince (or apple) into similar-sized chunks. Put roughly two-thirds of the olive oil in a bowl with the cinnamon and cumin, and season well with salt and pepper. Toss the squash in it, then place on a baking sheet. Put the remaining olive oil and the vinegar in another bowl, season well and toss the quince or apple in it. Place on another baking sheet. Roast both in the oven for 30–40 minutes, until they are completely tender but not falling apart (they may take slightly different cooking times, so test the flesh with a sharp knife).

Meanwhile, make the pipián. Prepare the ancho chillies as on page 86. When they are toasted, transfer them to a bowl with the de-stalked chiles de árbol and cover with boiling water. Soak for 10–15 minutes, until they are soft.

Toast the pumpkin seeds in a dry frying pan for 5–10 minutes, until they start to pop open and lightly colour, then set aside. In the same pan, toast the garlic cloves and onion over a high heat until both are blackened and charred and the garlic is soft, about 10 minutes…

Feeds 4–6
Time: 1 hour

2 squash (about 2kg)
2 large quinces or apples
100ml olive oil
½ teaspoon ground cinnamon
1 teaspoon freshly ground cumin
sea salt and freshly ground pepper
2 tablespoons red wine vinegar

For the pipián:
3 ancho chillies
2 chiles de árbol, de-stalked
120g pumpkin seeds
4 garlic cloves, unpeeled
1 large onion, chopped into large, rough chunks
700ml water or stock
2 large bunches of coriander, roughly chopped
large bunch of basil, roughly chopped
2 tablespoons cooking oil

Whiz the pumpkin seeds to a fine paste in a blender. Add the drained chillies, the onion and the garlic (slipped out of its skin) and whiz again with just enough water or stock to loosen the blades. Add the herbs and keep whizzing until you have a smooth paste.

Heat a flameproof casserole dish, pour in the cooking oil and, when shimmering hot, add the pumpkin seed paste. Stir-fry vigorously for a minute or so, being careful as it will spit. Gradually stir in the rest of the stock to make your sauce. Throw in the roasted pumpkin and quince and heat through for 10 minutes, seasoning generously with salt and pepper.

Serve your stew in deep, warm bowls. This is particularly good drizzled with Green herb oil (page 228).

Stuffed ancho chillies with refried beans and red onion marmalade

Carolyn (aka 'Truffer Lum') does all of Wahaca's buying and looks after our suppliers, our chefs and pretty much everyone else in the company, given half a chance. Occasionally, when I'm lucky, she accompanies me on trips to seek out ingredients and new recipes, a task that requires both energy and stamina, as we end up tasting and dissecting huge amounts of food. She is brilliant at it and an invaluable member of our team. We put these chillies on the menu at Wahaca after one such excursion to Mexico. We ate so much food that fortnight that we almost had to be rolled home, but we certainly returned brimming with ideas. This is a rich supper dish, so is best served with just a simple green salad and a little rice.

Cover the chillies with the boiling water and leave to soak for 15 minutes.

Meanwhile, make the marmalade. Melt the butter in a wide-bottomed casserole or deep frying pan and sweat the onions, allspice and thyme over a medium heat for 10 minutes, or until the onions are starting to colour at the edges. Season with plenty of salt and pepper and stir in the sugar. Cook for another 10–15 minutes, until the onions have caramelised and turned a deep, dark colour. Add the vinegar and wine and simmer for 5–10 minutes to reduce to a thick, syrupy sauce.

Preheat the oven to 130°C/250°F/gas 1. Once the chillies are soft, carefully drain away the water and make a slit down the side of them from stalk to tip. Rinse under running water to wash away all the seeds, then fill with scoops of refried beans. Arrange the chillies on a baking sheet and warm through in the oven for 5 minutes.

Meanwhile, peel the plantain and slice into long diagonal pieces; you should easily get 8 slices. Fry each slice in butter until golden and caramelised on each side. Serve each chilli with a few heaped tablespoons of the onion marmalade, a dollop of crème fraîche and a few slices of the fried plantain.

Feeds 4
Time: 45 minutes

4 ancho chillies
100ml boiling water
½ quantity Refried beans (page 148)
1 blackened plantain
butter, for frying
crème fraîche, to serve

For the red onion marmalade:
70g butter
500g red onions, finely sliced into half-moons
2 teaspoons allspice berries
leaves from 8–10 sprigs of thyme
sea salt and freshly ground black pepper
150g brown sugar
45ml sherry vinegar
150ml red wine

CORIANDER POTATOES

side

A little of this, a little of that: the purpose of side dishes is to complement food and add variety and interest to the plate. In Mexico this means beans, preferably lots of them, whether slow-cooked until soft to the bite or puréed smooth, flavoured with herbs and cooked in fat, mostly lard with all its wonderful flavour. Beans are one of life's delights, rich in protein and taste and wonderfully cheap. They form a completely balanced diet when matched with corn and chillies, thus making up the holy trinity of Mexico's staple ingredients.

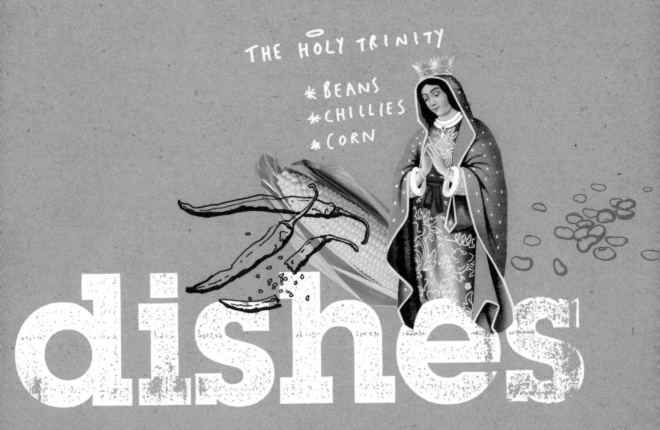

THE HOLY TRINITY

* BEANS
* CHILLIES
* CORN

dishes

Mexico is also full of wild herbs and greens, and these can be sautéd in butter or oil and served alongside the main courses, or used to fill tacos, tamales and gorditas. Simple to cook but packed full of goodness and taste, greens superbly complement a plate of Mexican food, especially in the depths of winter.

Potatoes and sweet potatoes, both native to the Americas, absorb flavour and heat, fill you up with good carbs, and are used in every kind of street food. Finally, there are lovely fresh salads, such as the feather-light Mexican summer slaw (page 142), billowing out over great steaming plates of slow-cooked meat. These refreshing counterbalances to meaty dishes exemplify the contrasts in flavour, texture and heat of classic Mexican cooking.

At Wahaca, our side dishes have always been hugely popular. In particular, the Refried beans (page 148) go with everything, taste out of this world and, aside from a little fat, are pretty good for you. At work, we like to snack on a bowl, dunking in warm-from-the-fryer tortilla chips. Definitely something to try at home!

Mexican summer slaw

Fresh, crunchy, colourful and bursting with flavour, this salad is a far cry from the slaw you migh find at cheap take-away joints. It is delicious served with slow-cooked meats or Sunday roasts, or as toppings for tacos and tostadas. It is delicious with anything for that matter!

Start by making the dressing. Lightly dry-roast the cumin seeds in a small frying pan for a minute or so to release their flavour, then grind to a powder.

In a small bowl, mix the egg yolk, mustard, garlic, cumin, salt, vinegar and lime juice, then gradually whisk in the olive oil. Stir in the sour cream, taste and add more seasoning if needed.

Toast the pumpkin seeds in a dry frying pan for a minute or so, until lightly coloured. In a large bowl, mix all the slaw ingredients together, but save some of the pumpkin seeds for garnish. About 10 minutes before you sit down to eat, toss the slaw with the dressing and sprinkle with the reserved pumpkin seeds.

Feeds 4
Time: 20 minutes

1 tablespoon pumpkin seeds
¼ firm white cabbage, finely sliced
small head of baby gem lettuce, finely sliced
6 large radishes, finely sliced
1 small red onion, finely sliced
1 large carrot, sliced into matchsticks
½ red chilli, finely sliced
2 tablespoons chopped fresh mint
1 tablespoon chopped fresh coriander

For the dressing:
1 teaspoon cumin seeds
1 egg yolk
½ teaspoon Dijon mustard
1 small garlic clove, crushed
large pinch of sea salt
2 teaspoons red wine vinegar
juice of ½ a lime
170ml extra virgin olive oil
1 tablespoon sour cream

Mexican green rice

This rice is served all over Mexico and is never off the menu at Wahaca. Its delicate flavour goes beautifully with fish or chicken, whilst its vivid, emerald green colour makes a pretty addition to any table of food.

Rinse the rice under cold water until the water runs clear. Place in a saucepan, cover with the stock or water, season well with salt and pepper and cook for about 20 minutes, until nearly tender.

Meanwhile, put the garlic, onion and herbs in a blender with a splash of water and whiz until you have a thick green purée. Heat the oil in a flameproof casserole pan and, when hot, add the purée and fry for 5 minutes, stirring so as not to burn.

Preheat the oven to 120°C/225°F/gas 1. Add the rice to the pan and stir well to combine. Cook for another few minutes, until most of the liquid has been absorbed. Check for seasoning, then cover with butter papers or greaseproof paper and a lid and put in the oven for 30 minutes to finish cooking. The rice can rest in the oven for up to 2 hours like this, so make it in advance if you like: it will be lovely, light and fluffy.

Feeds 6
Time: 30 minutes

400g basmati rice
600ml chicken or vegetable
    stock or water
sea salt and freshly ground
    black pepper
2 garlic cloves
1 medium onion
large handful of coriander
large bunch of parsley or
    spinach
2 tablespoons olive oil

Olive oil, lime and coriander potatoes

These potatoes are lovely with the Grilled sea bass on page 120. We have cooked them at countless Mexican events and they always go down a treat. Our recipe is adapted from one I found in my cooking bible, Diana Kennedy's *Essential Cuisines of Mexico*.

Soak the potatoes in water for 10 minutes to remove their starch, then drain and dry with a tea towel. Heat a large, wide-bottomed pan over a medium heat. Add the oil, heat for a few minutes, then add the potatoes. Season well with salt and pepper and stir-fry for 10 minutes, until some of the potatoes are starting to turn golden. Add the shallots, garlic and chillies and fry for a few more minutes, until the onion has softened.

Pour in the water and lime juice, cover the pan and bring to the boil. Turn the heat right down and cook until the water has been absorbed and the potatoes are cooked. Check the seasoning, take off the heat, add the coriander and a good glug of extra virgin olive oil and serve at once.

Feeds 4–6
Time: 40 minutes

700g new potatoes, sliced in half lengthways
3 tablespoons olive oil, plus extra for serving
sea salt and freshly ground black pepper
2 shallots, diced
2 garlic cloves, finely chopped
3 serrano chillies, finely chopped
200ml water
juice of 1 lime
large bunch of coriander leaves, roughly chopped

Sweet potato gratin with thyme, chilli and feta

At work we deep-fry sweet potatoes and drizzle them in our homemade Mojo de ajo (page 229) to create the most popular dish on our winter menu. This recipe is equally delicious but a little less fussy: we love the combination of smoky chipotles with the sweetness of the potato. It is similar to dauphinoise but cooked in a mixture of water and olive oil, which produces a wonderfully rich, comforting dish.

Preheat the oven to 210°C/410°F/gas 6.

Lightly grease a large baking dish or 2 small ones with olive oil. In a food processor, blitz together the chilli, feta, thyme, olive oil and stock (or water) and season the mixture well with salt and pepper. Do not worry about what this looks like – it will taste delicious!

Layer the sweet potato in the dish(es), interspersing each layer with the red onion and drizzles of the feta purée, seasoning each layer with more salt and pepper.

Cover with foil and bake for 45–50 minutes, or until until the sweet potato is completely soft in the middle, removing the foil halfway through the cooking so that the top becomes crisp and golden.

Feeds 4
Time: 1 hour

1–2 tablespoons Chipotles en adobo (page 238) or 1 teaspoon finely chopped chilli
150g feta cheese
big bunch of thyme, chopped
120ml olive oil
250ml vegetable stock or water
sea salt and freshly ground black pepper
3 large sweet potatoes, peeled and cut into 5mm slices
2 red onions, finely sliced

Refried beans

The ultimate comfort food, in Mexico these beans are served for breakfast, lunch and even with grilled lobster or langoustine for a smart dinner. They are called 'refrito', which means 'well fried', and this is the key. Cook them slowly in lots of lard or butter and you will taste their magic. This dish has been one of Wahaca's bestsellers since we opened our doors, and we always have huge simmering vats of beans ready to well fry!

If using dried beans, rinse them well and drain, picking out any loose pebbles. Cover with water and soak overnight to reduce the overall cooking time, and drain again (but if you don't have time don't worry – they will just take a little longer to cook). Place them in a large pan and cover with at least 10cm of cold water. Add the head of garlic, the herbs and the quartered onion and bring to the boil. Simmer the beans until they are just soft, about 2–3 hours, topping them up with boiling water if needs be, and skimming off any white foam that gathers on the surface.

Once soft, season the beans with plenty of sea salt and continue to cook for another 15–20 minutes so that the beans absorb the flavour. If you add the salt any sooner, it will prevent the beans from softening. Drain the cooked beans, reserving the cooking liquid but discarding the herbs, onion and garlic.

Feeds 4–6
Time: 25 minutes (unless using dried beans)

250g dried black beans or 600g tinned black beans, drained
head of garlic, cut in half, plus 2 extra cloves, chopped
3-4 bay leaves, fresh if possible
1 tablespoon chopped epazote or coriander root/stalks
2 medium onions, 1 quartered and 1 finely chopped
sea salt and freshly ground black pepper
at least 50g lard, butter or olive oil
few fresh bay leaves

To finish:
knob of butter
sour cream
50g Lancashire or Cheshire cheese, crumbled
freshly chopped coriander

Put the cooked beans, or the ones you have bought, into a blender and whiz to a smooth, thick purée, loosening it with either some of the cooking liquid or water.

Heat the fat in a heavy-bottomed pan and, when gently foaming, add the chopped onion. Season well with salt and pepper and sweat the onion until soft. Add the chopped garlic and cook for a further few minutes. Add the puréed beans to the onion and cook on a low heat for another 10 minutes, stirring constantly and adding more liquid from time to time if needed. The end result should be a smooth purée that falls easily from a wooden spoon. Check for seasoning as beans usually take quite a bit.

When you are ready to eat, stir in the knob of butter to make the beans shine, drizzle with the sour cream and scatter over the crumbled cheese and coriander. Serve with a bowl of Totopos (page 50) or tortilla crisps.

NOTE: If you haven't had time to soak the beans overnight, add 1/2 teaspoon bicarbonate of soda to help speed up the cooking process.

WHY NOT TRY? You can add chipotle or dried chilli flakes to the sweating onion to get spicy beans.

Black bean stew

A big pot of this stew makes a really delicious, cheap and nutritious supper – or you can serve it as a rich and satisfying side dish. It's a simple recipe, so you can play about with the ingredients: for example, replace the black beans with borlotti, pinto, cannellini or any other beans you can find; add chunks of pork and chorizo to make it even heartier; or leave out the bacon and use vegetable stock to make it meat-free.

Heat the olive oil in a large casserole pan over a medium heat. Add the bacon and cook until the lardons begin to brown slightly. Add the chopped onion, garlic, celery and carrots, stirring occasionally until the vegetables have softened (about 10–15 minutes). Add the cumin, allspice, thyme, oregano and chipotles and cook for a few more minutes. Next, add the plum tomatoes, crushing them a bit with a wooden spoon as you stir them in. Add the 2 remaining bay leaves and the cinnamon stick and bring to the boil. Reduce the heat to a low simmer and cook for about 40 minutes.

Add the cooked, drained beans and the stock, bring to the boil again, then lower the heat and simmer for a further 15–20 minutes. Remove from the heat and add the butter – this just gives a little more flavour and a shine to the sauce. Taste to check for seasoning. Garnish with sour cream or crème fraîche, the spring onions, coriander and slices of avocado or, if you prefer, grated Cheddar.

Feeds 6
Time: 90 minutes (unless using dried beans)

800g cooked black beans, tinned or homemade (see page 148)
1 large onion, quartered
2 tablespoons olive oil
200g unsmoked bacon lardons
1 onion, finely chopped
2 garlic cloves, crushed
3 sticks of celery, roughly chopped
2 carrots, peeled and roughly chopped
1 teaspoon ground cumin
pinch of allspice
small bunch each of thyme and oregano
1½ teapoons Chipotles en adobo (page 238)
2 x 400g tins plum tomatoes
1 small cinnamon stick
250ml beef or chicken stock
knob of butter
sea salt and freshly ground black pepper

To garnish:
sour cream or crème fraîche
3 spring onions, finely sliced
freshly chopped coriander
sliced avocado or grated Cheddar cheese

Spinach al mojo de ajo

Mojo de ajo is a glorious sauce made by slowly cooking garlic in oil until it is soft, sweet and unctuous. Its rich, delicious flavour goes beautifully with the minerally taste of all sorts of different greens, so experiment with whatever you can find in your local market or greengrocer's.

Discard any large stems from the spinach. Wash the leaves thoroughly in cold water, then drain for a few minutes in a colander.

Heat a large pan over a high heat and add the butter. When it is sizzling, add the spinach in 3 batches, stirring each time so that it wilts down and leaves space for more. Season with salt and pepper and stir for about 5 minutes, until the spinach has cooked down.

Squeeze over the lime juice and drizzle with the Mojo de ajo. Serve at once.

Feeds 4–6
Time: 5 minutes

700g fresh spinach
30g butter
sea salt and freshly ground
  black pepper
squeeze of lime
6–7 tablespoons Mojo de ajo
  (page 229)

Mexican winter salad

The glowing bright hues of pomegranate, radish and orange make this a truly beautiful salad. Light and refreshing, it's a lovely side dish with grilled chicken or fish, or makes a fabulous, light starter.

Whisk the dressing ingredients together and set aside.

Cut the peel and pith off the oranges. Slice the flesh thinly and put into a large bowl with all the other salad ingredients, apart from a few of the totopos and pomegranate seeds. Pour in the dressing and mix gently. Scatter the reserved totopos and pomegranate seeds over the salad before serving.

TIP: To remove pomegranate seeds easily, cut the fruit in half, hold it cut-side down over a bowl and tap the skin firmly with a wooden spoon. The seeds will simply drop out.

Feeds 4
Time: 15 minutes

sea salt
2 oranges
2 heads of fennel, trimmed and
 finely sliced
1 small red onion, finely sliced
1 red chilli, finely sliced (de-
 seeded if you like)
6 large radishes, finely sliced
seeds from 1 small
 pomegranate
small bunch of coriander,
 roughly chopped
50g feta cheese, crumbled
Totopos (page 50), cut into little
 strips

For the dressing:
juice of 1 lime
pinch of sugar
sea salt and freshly ground
 black pepper
100ml extra virgin olive oil

BUÑUELOS

VANILLA

If the Mexicans and the British have one thing in common – other than a love of beer and pork scratchings – it is their sweet tooth.

As lunch starts so late in Mexico, I have on occasion found myself ravenous in the middle of the day and, being of a naturally greedy disposition, delicacies like peanut brittle, walnut marzipan and amaranth candies prove irresistible at times like this. I have also developed an addiction to the strange-tasting salt-chilli tamarind and

mango sweets, which are sold on street-side stalls everywhere. They are insanely good and send our Mexican chefs quite giddy with delight if you bring a bag back to hand out.

The markets are full of ice cream stalls and carts, offering the perfect ice to cool you down and quench your thirst. Flavours range from the exotic (zapote fruit, zamorra, mamey, piña, papaya and tuna) to the luxurious (burnt cream, cajeta, vanilla and chocolate). At work we have a version of the cajeta (page 174), which is rich, caramelised and dotted with pieces of dark chocolate. But the classic Vanilla (page 158) is still our bestseller and, given that vanilla originates in Mexico, we highly

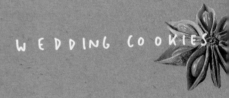

dings

approve. After some experimentation, we also came up with a Homemade vanilla essence (page 151), which is stupidly good drizzled onto any kind of pudding, and makes the most amazing present if poured into small bottles and prettily labelled.

In the cantinas, Italian-inspired pastries vie for attention with ricotta cakes (page 171) and chocolate puds, jellies, churros, rich creamy flans, rice puddings and crème brûlées (page 164).

But it is not simply sugar that is used to meet sweet cravings. Agave syrup, harvested from the same plant that produces tequila, is used to sweeten amaranth granolas and upmarket puddings. Exquisite organic honeys are

also popular, their delightfully floral taste courtesy of the bright-coloured flowers that spring up in every nook and cranny of the beautiful Mexican countryside. Piloncillo, a richly flavoured unrefined cane sugar, gives such a deep taste to food that I bring some back every time I visit and use it in both puddings and savoury dishes.

Even if you don't think you like sugar, here are sweets to tempt the palate and see off the sourest critics!

MANGOES

PASSION FRUIT
CRÈME BRÛLÉE

Homemade vanilla essence

I first made my own vanilla essence when I came back from the rainforests in Papantla, Veracruz, armed with the biggest bag of vanilla pods you have ever seen. Mexico is the birthplace of vanilla. The bean is the fruit of a thick green orchid vine that grows wild on the edge of the tropical forests, and seeing it in its natural habitat, where the stamens are carefully laid out to dry in the sun after they are picked, is a real inspiration. No wonder it is such an expensive spice (second only to saffron)! If you come across the pods on your travels, or buy too many from your local delicatessen, this recipe is a great way to preserve their bewitching, aromatic flavour.

Slit each vanilla pod lengthways along one side and almost all the way to the tip so that it remains in one piece. Pour a capful of vodka out of the bottle to make room for the pods and put them inside. Seal tightly and store in a dark place for 2–3 months, until the vodka has become a dark, rich caramel colour and radiates the smell of vanilla. Use in cocktails, beef dishes or puddings.

TIP: Homemade vanilla makes a lovely present. Just decant it into small bottles (you can buy these online), then seal and label them. Your friends will have a unique product that is delicious added to virtually any pudding.

Makes a bottle
Time: 2–3 months maturing

1 x 750ml bottle best-quality vodka
6 fresh, fat vanilla pods

A lovely vanilla ice cream, served 2 ways...

This a really simple recipe that makes a lot of ice cream, with no need for an ice cream machine. It's fantastic as it stands, especially if you make it with Homemade vanilla essence, but why not use it to make the variations below and opposite? The first combines two classic Mexican ingredients, peanuts and vanilla, while the second simply drowns the ice cream in coffee or liqueur or whatever you fancy. Either way, there's plenty to enjoy!

Put the egg yolks into a large bowl and whisk until light and fluffy. Combine the sugar with the water in a small, heavy-bottomed saucepan, stir over a medium heat until the sugar is completely dissolved, then boil the syrup until it reaches the 'thread' stage (around 108°C/225°F). It should look thick and syrupy, and the last drops poured from a metal spoon should form thin threads.

Pour the hot syrup onto the yolks in a steady stream, whisking all the time and not worrying if some of the syrup flies off in all directions. It happens! Add the vanilla ssence and continue to whisk until you have a thick, creamy white mousse. Whip the double cream until thick and smooth and gently fold it into the mousse. Pour into two plastic boxes, then cover and freeze.

Feeds 8–10
Time: 1 hour + 2–3 hours freezing

4 egg yolks
100g caster sugar
250ml water
1 teaspoon vanilla essence, ideally homemade (page 157)
750ml double cream

For the peanut praline:
110g skinned, unsalted peanuts
110g caster sugar

For the affogato:
1 shot espresso per person

Peanut praline ice cream

Preheat the oven to 180°C/350°F/gas 4. Roast the peanuts on a baking sheet for about 5 minutes or until they have turned a pale golden brown colour. Set aside.

To make the praline, melt the sugar in a heavy-bottomed saucepan over a medium heat, but do not stir or you will get into a terrible mess! Instead, as the sugar starts turning a deep caramel colour in patches, lower the heat and swirl the pan around gently to disperse the darker patches amongst the still unmelted sugar. When completely melted, add the peanuts and carefully rotate the pan until all the nuts are covered with caramel. Pour onto a baking sheet lined with greaseproof paper and allow to cool.

When the praline is set, crush with a rolling pin or in a food processor – the texture should be quite coarse and gritty.

After about 1½ hours, when the ice cream is just beginning to set, fold 4 tablespoons of the praline into one of the containers and freeze again. Be careful – if you fold it in too early, the praline will sink to the bottom.

Serve the ice cream scattered with a little of the extra praline and, if you like, the mangoes on page 160.

Affogato

Affogato means 'drowned', so if you've saved a container of ice cream, why not try this Mexico City favourite – vanilla ice cream drowned in the liquid of your choice? Simply serve each guest a glass of ice cream with a small shot of espresso and let them do the rest.

Mangoes in anise-chilli syrup

Mangoes are found all over Mexico during the long summer months. At the same time of year in Britain we are spoilt too, with Alphonso mangoes in season, as well as the wonderful honey mangoes from Pakistan. I always go to the market for mangoes as they are so much better than the green ones in the supermarket, which never really ripen. Worth making a trip for. I love to serve them chilled in this spicy, fresh syrup, and added to the Peanut praline ice cream (page 158) they're glorious. The tequila adds a wonderfully complex note, producing a magic flavour combination for a hot summer's day.

Skin and dice the mangoes and place in a bowl. Put the agave syrup, lime zest and juice, star anise, chilli and tequila into a small pan and bring to simmering point. Simmer gently for 5 minutes, then turn off the heat, allowing the mixture to cool and infuse with all the flavours.

When the syrup is cool, pour it over the mangoes and allow to marinate for 45 minutes in the fridge. Serve with scoops of ice cream and torn mint leaves scattered over the mango.

Feeds 4
Time: 10 minutes + 45 minutes marinating

2 fat ripe mangoes
60g agave syrup
zest and juice of 2 limes
1 star anise
1 red chilli, de-seeded and finely chopped
2 tablespoons tequila

To serve:
good-quality vanilla ice cream
small handful of torn mint leaves

Handkerchief puffs with spiced apple purée

I first came across these puffs in a street market in Oaxaca, but soon noticed them all over the country, either filled with fruit purées or oozing luxurious pastry creams. They are a testament to Mexico's love of sweet things and are amazing served with thick clotted cream.

Roll out the pastry into 2 big squares about 3mm thick. Trim and straighten the edges with a very sharp knife, then cut each piece of dough into 5 equal squares.

Place the squares on baking sheets lined with baking paper, then refrigerate for at least 1 hour. They can be frozen at this stage if desired.

Meanwhile, put the apple, brandy, lemon juice, sugar, butter and spices in a saucepan and gently cook until the apple softens and most of the liquid has evaporated, about 10–15 minutes.

When you are ready to bake the puffs, preheat the oven to 190°C/375°F/gas 5 and remove the pastry from the fridge. Place on a work surface with the corners of the pastry in the shape of a diamond. Spoon small amounts of the purée onto the lower half of the diamond, leaving a 5mm border. Brush this with a little egg wash, then fold the upper half of the pastry over the purée to make a triangle and seal the edges with a fork.

When you are ready to cook them, brush the top of the pastries with beaten egg and prick them a few times with a fork to allow the steam to escape. Sprinkle with granulated sugar and bake in the oven for 15–20 minutes, or until golden brown.

Makes 9–10
Time: 1 hour + at least 1 hour chilling

1 x 500g packet all butter puff pastry
3 large cooking apples, peeled, cored and cut into 1cm dice
1 tablespoon brandy
juice of ½ a lemon
2 tablespoons caster sugar
15g butter
pinch of ground allspice
½ teaspoon cinnamon
1 egg, beaten
granulated sugar, to sprinkle

SPOON A LITTLE PURÉE ONTO THE LOWER HALF OF THE DIAMOND, LEAVING A SMALL BORDER...

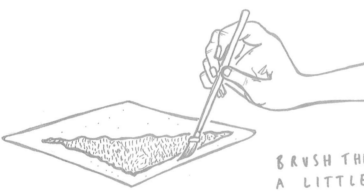

BRUSH THE BORDER WITH A LITTLE EGGWASH...

FOLD PASTRY OVER, SEAL EDGES, THEN BRUSH TOP AND PRICK WITH A FORK.

Passion fruit crème brûlée

These brûlées are so good that I could probably eat several in one sitting. The sharp, citrusy flavour of the passion fruit beautifully offsets the richness of the cream. This is one for impressing the in-laws.

Preheat the oven to 150°C/300°F/gas 2. Cut the passion fruit in half and scoop out the seeds. Pour just over half of them into a small saucepan together with 3 tablespoons of the sugar and a tablespoon of water. Gently heat the mix until it begins to bubble. After a few minutes it will begin to thicken and become syrupy and golden. Divide the syrup between 6 ramekins, making sure it covers the bottom.

In a large bowl, whisk together the egg yolks and sugar until the mixture is pale and creamy (much easier to do with an electric whisk, but perhaps not as satisfying).

Now heat the cream, milk, remaining passion fruit, vanilla pod and lime zest in a saucepan over a low heat. When hot but *not* boiling, remove from the heat and scrape the vanilla seeds into the cream, discarding the pod. Gradually pour the cream into the egg mixture, whisking briskly as you pour to stop the eggs from scrambling. Strain the mixture through a sieve into a large jug.

Place the ramekins in a roasting tin and pour the custard into each one to cover the passion fruit base. Pour enough boiling water into the tin to come about halfway up the side of the ramekins, then carefully place on the middle shelf of the oven. Bake for about 20 minutes, or until the custard is set but still wobbly when gently touched. Remove from the oven and allow to cool before chilling in the fridge, ideally overnight, but at least for 2 hours.

Sprinkle each ramekin evenly with a 1mm layer of sugar. Using a blowtorch, melt and caramelise the sugar until it has turned a dark amber colour and the surface is completely glazed. (This could be done under a hot grill if you don't have a blowtorch.) Cool again before serving.

Feeds 6
Time: 90 minutes + at least 2 hours chilling

12 passion fruit
6 egg yolks
150g caster sugar, plus extra for the topping
300ml double cream
45ml milk
1 vanilla pod, split open lengthways
zest of ½ a lime (use a potato peeler so you get large strips)

NOTE: You will need 6 ramekins (approx. 4cm deep and 8cm wide) and (if possible) a cooks' blowtorch.

Summer fruit nieve

Nieve (nee-eh-vey) means 'snow' and is the Mexican equivalent of granita. It has a coarse, icy texture, is a doddle to make and doesn't need any fancy equipment. Nieves make the perfect pudding on hot days. In fact, they are so good that I make masses at a time and keep them in the freezer, either for a ready-made end to a dinner party or as an impromptu cocktail, blitzed with lashings of tequila. Children love it too, but perhaps leave out the tequila…

In a small, heavy-bottomed saucepan gently heat 150g of the sugar and the water. When the sugar has dissolved, boil for a couple of minutes. Remove from the heat and set aside.

In a food processor or blender, purée the summer berries with the remaining sugar, then sieve for a smoother texxture. Add the sugar syrup along with the cassis, tequila and lime juice and stir well.

Pour the mixture into a shallow, freezer-proof container or tray, and freeze for 1–2 hours, until partially frozen. Remove the nieve from the freezer and use a fork to break up any ice crystals that are forming. Return to the freezer and leave for another 1–2 hours, then fork again. Repeat the process until you have a rough-textured sorbet.

Serve with double cream or, if you are a real sophisticat, more tequila poured over the top!

Feeds about 8
Time: 25 minutes + 3–4 hours freezing

200g caster sugar
150ml water
150g raspberries
200g strawberries
150g blackberries
1 tablespoon crème de cassis
1 tablespoon reposado tequila
juice of 1 lime

To serve:
double cream
tequila (optional)

Buñuelos

Light, mouth-watering wafers of deep-fried dough sprinkled with caster sugar, buñuelos are found in cantinas throughout Mexico, usally served with tropical fruit or very sweet fruit purées. I love them with this fresh raspberry sauce, but they are equally good with cherry, blackberry, strawberry or redcurrant sauce, depending on your fancy and the time of year.

Put the twice-sifted flour into a large bowl and add the sugar, baking powder and salt. In a separate bowl, whisk the milk, egg and crushed anise until frothy.

Make a well in the centre of the flour and gradually whisk in the milk mixture, using your hands to bring it all together into a dough. On a floured surface, knead the dough for 5–10 minutes. Shape into approximately 18 balls (25g each). Cover with a cloth and rest for 20 minutes.

Meanwhile, make the purée by whizzing the raspberries and sugar in a blender or food processor, then push the mixture through a sieve. If you like, you can sharpen the purée with a squeeze of lemon and a dash of cassis.

Roll each dough ball on a lightly floured surface into very thin rounds 10–15cm in diameter. Leave to stand for 5 minutes.

In a large, deep frying pan, heat the sunflower oil until it is hot enough to make a cube of bread sizzle when you add it. Fry the dough circles like pancakes, one at a time, until puffed and golden brown on both sides, turning them only once or they will become soggy. Drain well on kitchen paper and sprinkle with sugar whilst they are still warm.

Put 1 or 2 on each plate, not minding at all if they break as it looks all the more rustic. Add a scoop of vanilla ice cream, a scattering of berries and a generous spoonful of raspberry purée. Eat up greedily!

Feeds 8
Time: about 30 minutes

280g plain flour, sifted twice
1 tablespoon caster sugar, plus
    extra to sprinkle
½ teaspoon baking powder
¼ teaspoon salt
125ml milk
1 large egg
½ teaspoon anise seeds,
    crushed in a mortar
375ml sunflower oil, for frying

For the raspberry purée:
500g raspberries
75g caster sugar
squeeze of lemon juice
    (optional)
dash of crème de cassis
    (optional)

To serve:
good-quality vanilla ice cream
summer berries

Chocolate and cinnamon parfait

This is quite the deadliest, most dangerously delectable dessert I have ever made. Spoonfuls of it will drive you wild for more. An extra helping will win you friends for life. It takes some time to prepare, so set aside a relaxed morning or afternoon to make it, and consider it time well spent.

Cover the sugar with the boiling water and stir to dissolve. Set aside 50ml and store the rest in the fridge for making margaritas (page 207). Stir in the vanilla essence.

Put the cocoa powder, cinnamon and salt in a non-stick saucepan, add a tiny bit of the reserved sugar syrup and stir vigorously with a wooden spoon or silicon whisk, slowly adding enough of the remaining syrup to produce a smooth chocolate paste. Gradually stir in the rest of the sugar syrup over a gentle heat, stirring from time to time until the cocoa comes up to simmering point, about 15 minutes. Simmer, stirring all the time, for 5 minutes before taking the mixture off the heat and adding the chocolate. Stir until the chocolate has completely melted, then cool until it feels lukewarm on your lip.

Feeds about 8
Time: 90 minutes + 2 hours freezing

350g sugar
350ml boiling water
1 tablespoon vanilla essence, preferably homemade (page 157)
6 tablespoons cocoa powder
½ teaspoon ground cinnamon
good pinch of sea salt
100g dark chocolate (at least 60% cocoa solids), broken into small pieces
8 egg yolks
500ml double cream
4 tablespoons añejo (aged) tequila or dark rum

In the meantime, put the egg yolks into a mixer and whisk for 5–10 minutes, until they are pale and fluffy. Now whisk in the chocolate mix, little by little, until it is fully incorporated. Be careful – if you add it too quickly, it will scramble the yolks. Transfer the mixture to a bowl suspended over a pan of simmering water, or if you have a sensitive electric hob you can cook it directly over a very low heat. Stir until thick enough to coat the back of a wooden spoon, or has reached 85°C/185°F. Make sure you stir continuously so that the eggs don't scramble.

Transfer the chocolate syrup back to the mixer and whisk on full speed for 1 minute, on medium speed for 4 minutes and on low speed for 5 minutes, until it has thickened and increased in volume. Transfer to a large bowl and cool in a sink of iced cold water for at least 30 minutes.

Once the chocolate syrup has cooled, whip the cream to soft peaks (be careful not to overwhip). Fold a quarter of the cream into the chocolate syrup and when that's fully incorporated, fold in another quarter. Fold in the tequila or rum and then the rest of the cream until you have a smooth mixture.

Transfer to a shallow freezer-proof container, cover and freeze for at least 2 hours. Remove from the freezer 20 minutes before serving. This ice cream is so rich that unless your friends are serious chocaholics, they will want only small bowlfuls.

Wickedly dark chocolate mousse

I am a confirmed chocolate addict, and perhaps one of the reasons why I love Mexico so much is because it is the land of the brilliant cocoa bean. This mousse harnesses all the rich, deep, velvety smoothness of dark chocolate and illustrates why some women prefer it to almost anything else!

Whisk the egg yolks and sugar together on a high speed for at least 5 minutes, or until the yolks have thickened to the consistency of double cream.

In the meantime, break up the chocolate and put it in a heatproof bowl with the butter. Set over a pan of gently simmering water, ensuring that the bowl doesn't actually touch it or the chocolate may burn. Stir the chocolate until melted and smooth, then stir in the coffee.

Carefully stir the yolks into the melted chocolate and, when they are fully incorporated, add the booze (if using).

Whisk the egg whites with the salt until they form stiff peaks and do not move when you turn the bowl upside down. Using a large, metal spoon, fold a small amount of the egg white into the chocolate mixture to loosen it, then carefully fold in the rest. Be careful not to stir too much or you will beat the air out of the egg white.

Pour the mixture into small glasses and put in the fridge for a few hours or overnight. Serve on its own or with cold double cream for pouring on top.

Feeds 6
Time: 40 minutes + at least 2 hours chilling

6 large eggs, separated
50g caster sugar
200g dark chocolate (about 70% cocoa solids)
50g unsalted butter
2 tablespoons very strong black coffee (preferably espresso)
large glug of good tequila or dark rum (optional, but so good)
pinch of sea salt
double cream, to serve (optional)

Vanilla, lime and ricotta cake

Requesón is a fresh curd cheese that is used extensively in Mexican cooking (the closest equivalent in the UK is ricotta). It makes the most incredible cake, especially when paired with vanilla and fresh lime. This is great at teatime or as a smart pudding.

Preheat the oven to 150°C/300°F/gas 2. Butter a 24cm springform cake tin and line it with greaseproof paper.

Toast the almonds in the oven for about 10 minutes, until they turn a pale golden colour. Finely chop them or pulse in a food processor; they should resemble small breadcrumbs rather than flour. Combine them with the flour and lime zest.

Cream the butter with the sugar until pale and fluffy. Beat in the vanilla essence and the egg yolks, one by one. Stir in the flour mixture.

In a separate bowl, beat the ricotta with a fork and whisk in the lime juice. Gradually fold this into the butter mixture.

Beat the egg whites until they form stiff peaks and do not move when you turn the bowl upside down. Using a large metal spoon, fold a little of the egg white into the cake mixture to loosen it, then fold in the remainder.

Bake in the preheated oven for about 1 hour, until just set when you press gently on the surface. Let the cake cool in its tin for 5–10 minutes before turning onto a wire rack to finish cooling.

Feeds 10
Time: 2 hours

225g unsalted butter, softened, plus extra for greasing
300g blanched almonds
65g plain flour
grated zest of 6 limes and juice of 6–8 limes (about 175ml)
250g golden caster sugar
2 tablespoons vanilla essence
6 eggs, separated
300g ricotta cheese

Mexican wedding cookies

My great friend Claire Ptak (aka 'Claire Cakes) made these crumbly, feather-light sandwich cookies for my wedding. The cajeta caramel filling is glorious, but if you're pushed for time, you could use ready-made dulce de leche, a rich caramel sauce, instead.

Cream together the butter, sugar and salt, then mix in the flour until a dough just starts to form, 1–2 minutes at the most. The less you work the dough, the lighter your cookies will be. Work in the rum, orange zest and walnuts.

Divide the dough into two equal pieces and lightly roll them on a clean work surface into neat logs about 3cm in diameter. Using a sharp knife, cut the logs into 5mm discs. Lay these out on non-stick baking sheets and freeze for 30 minutes. Meanwhile, preheat the oven to 170°C/335°F/gas 3 and place the icing sugar in a big bowl.

Bake the chilled discs for about 20 minutes, by which time they will have set but not taken on any colour. Toss them quickly in the icing sugar, then leave to cool on wire racks. Don't worry if the icing sugar melts a little.

When cooled, spread half the cookies with the caramel, then sandwich with the other halves, pressing gently to ensure an even spread. Sprinkle the finished sandwiches with extra icing sugar so that they are snowy white. Enjoy immediately or store in airtight containers.

Makes about 24 cookies
Time: 1 hour + 30 minutes chilling

225g unsalted butter, softened
70g caster sugar
small pinch of salt
310g plain flour
1 tablespoon dark rum
zest of ½ an orange
100g walnuts, roughly chopped
approx. 350g icing sugar, plus extra to sprinkle
150g Homemade cajeta (page 174), or dulce de leche (available online)

Homemade cajeta

Cajeta (kah-heh-tah) is a deliciously rich goats' milk caramel. Majestic with the Mexican wedding cookies (page 172), it also works brilliantly drizzled over crêpes, tortillas, ice cream or fruit. There's a fair bit of standing and stirring involved here, but you can happily while away the time chatting to a friend (just make sure they bring a small container to take some sauce away with them).

In a large, heavy-bottomed saucepan, combine the milk, sugar, vanilla and salt over a medium heat. Bring to the boil, stirring frequently to dissolve the sugar. Meanwhile, dissolve the bicarbonate of soda in a tablespoon of cold water.

Remove the milk from the heat and rapidly stir in the bicarb. The mixture will really bubble up, so be ready to blow it if you think it's going to spill over the sides. When the bubbles subside, return the pan to the heat.

Now simmer the mixture for 1 hour, stirring occasionally, until it has turned a soft caramel colour. At this stage you may need to turn the heat down a little and stir more frequently to prevent the mixture from catching and burning. As it simmers, the cajeta will thicken and turn a rich caramel-brown. Test for readiness by spooning a small droplet into a glass of cold water: if a soft ball forms, the mixture is ready. Stir in the rum and remove from the heat.

Once cooled, the cajeta will become stiff and difficult to spoon. Simply warm it up again, adding milk or hot water, 1 teaspoon at a time until you have the desired syrupy consistency.

Serve warm as you like, or refrigerate in a sterilised jar for up to 6 months.

NOTE: To sterilise glass containers and lids, wash them in a very hot dishwasher or boil in a pan of water for 10 minutes. Allow to dry before use.

Makes 1 x 450g jar
Time: 70–80 minutes

1 litre goats' milk
220g caster sugar
1 tablespoon vanilla essence
good pinch of sea salt
½ teaspoon bicarbonate of soda
1 tablespoon dark rum

Grilled pineapple with toasted coconut flakes and dark caramel

This pudding is sweetly sinful and gratifyingly easy to prepare. The flavour of grilled pineapple is perfectly paired with intense dark caramel, and the crisp, toasted coconut provides a lovely crunch.

Toast the coconut flakes in a dry frying pan until they have become a lovely pale golden colour all over. Set aside.

Now make the caramel. Pour the water into a pan, add the sugar and melt without stirring over a medium heat. Simmer briskly until the caramel starts to turn a deep golden colour. Swirl the pan to distribute the darker parts of the sugar and continue to cook until the sugar is a deep, dark brown. Its slightly burnt flavour will offset the sweetness of the caramel.

Add the rum, lime juice and cream and stir vigorously, being careful as the caramel will rise up and splutter a little. Season with a pinch of salt.

Heat a griddle pan or frying pan. Brush the melted butter onto the pineapple slices and griddle or fry them until caramelised and golden on both sides.

Divide the grilled pineapple between your serving plates, then pour a little of the warm syrup over each serving, followed by scoops of ice cream or a dollop of double cream. Pour more of the caramel on top and sprinkle with the toasted coconut flakes.

TIP: When choosing pineapples, sniff the bottom end for the sweet fresh scent that will tell you it's ready to eat.

Feeds 6–8
Time: 30 minutes

30g large coconut flakes
25g butter, melted
1 ripe pineapple, peeled and
  cut into 5–6 slices
good-quality vanilla ice cream
  or thick double cream

For the caramel:
130ml water
200g caster sugar
4 tablespoons dark rum
juice of 2 limes
3 tablespoons cold double
  cream
pinch of sea salt

fiesta

It is fair to say that we like a good party at Wahaca. We held our first Christmas party in the restaurant at Covent Garden and it was so wild that some of the team were seen still staggering about the next morning.

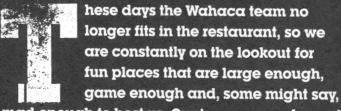

These days the Wahaca team no longer fits in the restaurant, so we are constantly on the lookout for fun places that are large enough, game enough and, some might say, mad enough to host us. Our team comes from all four corners of the globe: Mexico, Spain, India, eastern Europe, Africa, China, Brazil, the Middle East and even some from Blighty. This wonderful mix of people makes for a heady cocktail, particularly on the dance floor, where the moves are as eclectic as they are electric. One day we may even be allowed to realise our ambition to dress up as skeletons and do the *Thriller* dance sequence.

Of course, tequila is a drink that was born for parties. Never was there a spirit that so inspired the foot to twitch and the hips to shake. Our last staff trip to Mexico bore testament to this. As we were there to try as many of the local dishes as possible, we slightly overdid the late lunches, and in the evenings we were happy to stay away from dining rooms and head for the local bars instead. We indulged in relay races of carousing, with most of us incapable of managing more than a few nights partying over the week. Apart from Elki and Julio, that is, who both have the constitution of an ox and were happily dancing every night, delighted to be back in their home country.

Although Margaritas (page 207) proved very popular with our bunch, particularly when sweetened with the super-healthy and delicious agave syrup and flavoured with lime, tamarind, passion fruit or hibiscus flowers, we discovered that in Mexico the style is to sip tequila with a glass of Sangrita (page 210) on the side. Beers are also hugely popular, either straight up or served with the juice of 1 fresh lime and a salt rim.

Our next trip is fast approaching, and this time we are planning to include a trip to the beach. What we eat and drink there will have to be the subject of another book!

STUFFED CHILLIES

PORK SCRATCHINGS

SOFT-BAKED FETA

nibl

Old-school bars in Mexico always have a selection of salty, delicious nibbles to munch on with drinks. We love the Addictive hot chilli nuts (page 195) that we guzzled up in every bar we visited, and Pork scratchings (page 190) became our guilty pleasure. In Mexico they are served with ice-cold beer and freshly made Guacamole (page 194), which is a phenomenal combination. Serve this to your friends at the weekend before lunch and wait for the compliments to come flooding in.

bles

FRESHLY MASHED AVOCADO

I am never sure whether the aim with these bar snacks is to encourage a greater thirst for beer and tequila or to help line the stomach, enabling one to stand upright for longer. However you treat them, they are great fun to make at home (handily, most of the work can be done in advance) and even more fun to eat.

Think of fried sweet Plantain and chorizo (page 183) or a Soft-baked feta dip (page 188) scented with herbs and garlic. This is the ultimate party food and a world away from cocktail sausages. Pick a handful of recipes from this chapter, forget the formal courses and enjoy your own fiesta at home!

ADDICTIVE HOT CHILLI NUTS

Plantain
and chorizo

Happiness is ... sweet fried plantain with chewy, salty chorizo! These nibbles are the ultimate party food, a hundred times more irresistible than mini sausages and a thousand times more original. Use plantains that have blackening skin to make sure they are sweet, not starchy. If they are still yellow/green when you buy them, simply stash in a paper bag and leave to ripen somewhere warm.

Cut the chorizo diagonally into oval slices about 2cm thick. Cut the plantain into similar oval slices, but 5mm thicker so that they keep their shape in the frying pan.

Put your extractor fan on full and heat a heavy-bottomed frying pan over a medium flame until it is smoking hot. Brush the pan with a tiny slick of oil, just enough to lightly grease the bottom, and add enough chorizo to make a single layer, with enough space to flip the slices. Turn the heat down to medium-high and fry on each side until they have taken colour and are crisping on the outside, about 5–10 minutes. Transfer to a plate lined with kitchen paper and fry the remaining slices, pouring away the excess fat into a small earthenware bowl as you go. This fat has amazing flavour, so cover and store in the fridge for cooking.

When all the chorizo is cooked, put some of the fat back into the pan and, still over a medium heat, fry the plantain slices on both sides until they are golden brown and caramelised and have cooked all the way through, about 5–10 minutes. Cut them in half so they are about the same size as the chorizo slices.

Grab a helper and the cocktail sticks and spear first a slice of green chilli, then a plantain slice and finally a chorizo slice (the chorizo slice goes last as it stops everything else from sliding off the sticks). Arrange them willy-nilly on a serving plate, the chorizo at the bottom, and watch them disappear.

Feeds 8–10
Time: 30 minutes

400g good-quality chorizo
oil, for frying
3 plantains
2 fresh green chillies, very
    thinly sliced

NOTE: You will need cocktail sticks.

TIP: You can keep the plantain and chorizo slices warm in a low oven as you cook each batch. Or if you're really organised, you can fry the lot ahead of time, then warm in the oven at 170°C/335°F/gas 3 for about 10 minutes before you skewer and serve them.

Plantain boats

We take a dozen of our staff for a foodie-packed tour of Mexico every other year, and it is an enormous treat to discover new recipes and eat so much wonderful food. We meet some of Mexico's greatest chefs, as well as street-food sellers; all of them seem to treat us like family.

We learnt how to make these Plantain boats with the wondrous chef Margarita Carrillo. They're delectable drizzled with our Head chef's garlic and adobo sauce (page 241) and double cream, or you can serve them with a spicy tomato sauce and plain rice as a main course. If you want to mix things up a bit, stuff the plantain with chorizo or Chilorio (page 115) – both work beautifully.

Chop the tops and bottoms off the plantain, then cut them in half. Cover the pieces in cold water and bring to the boil, simmering over a medium heat until the flesh is soft, about 45 minutes. The skins usually split open but don't worry about that. Once cooked, skin, drain and cool, then put the plantain in a food processor with the flour, season generously with salt and process to a smooth paste.

Mix the ricotta with the grated pecorino and season with a little salt and lots of black pepper. Chop the thyme leaves and stir into the cheese mix.

Feeds 8
Time: 80 minutes

3 large plantains (about 750g)
4 tablespoons plain flour
sea salt
170g ricotta cheese
20g pecorino cheese, grated
leaves from small handful of
  thyme sprigs
freshly ground black pepper
sunflower oil, for frying

Pour a 2cm depth of sunflower oil into a frying pan and put over a low heat. Wet your hands with cold water and divide the plantain mixture into 8 balls. Wet your hands again (this will miraculously stop the dough from sticking) and press out each ball into an oblong shape about 5–8mm thick that covers most of your hand. Press a long groove down the middle of each pancake and spoon in about a tablespoon of the cheese mix. Roll up so that the cheese mixture is completely enclosed.

Dust the plantain boats fairly generously with flour, then fry 2 at a time over a medium heat, turning carefully to stop them sticking. If they are browning too quickly, turn the heat down a little. Drain on kitchen paper.

Serve straight away, or set aside for later, in which case reheat in a medium oven (about 170°C/335°F/gas 3). This will give you a chance to fumigate the kitchen of frying smells, and the plantain boats will also release a bit more fat, which you can pat away with more kitchen paper.

WHY NOT TRY? These are delicious served with the Spicy pumpkin seed spread on page 187.

Mexican crudités with chilli-lime salt

This is a heavenly dish to nibble when the weather is hot and you need something to quench your thirst. Serve with drinks, or enjoy as a light breakfast after a heavy night.

Grind all the chilli salt ingredients to a fine powder.

Cut the cucumber lengthways into quarters, spoon out the seeds, then cut the flesh into thick wedges.

Arrange all the fruit and vegetables fetchingly on a large plate, then squeeze over the lime juice. Serve with a small pot of the chilli salt to dip the crudités into.

Feeds 4
Time: 15 minutes

1 cucumber, peeled
1 bunch of radishes, trimmed
  and scrubbed
2 ripe mangoes, peeled and
  cut into wedges
1 watermelon, peeled and
  cubed
juice of 1 lime

For the chilli salt:
2 tablespoons sea salt
4 chiles de arbol or 8 small
  dried red chillies
zest of 3 limes
2 tablespoons caster sugar
¼ teaspoon cumin seeds

Spicy pumpkin seed spread

Chunky, fragrant and deliciously spicy, this is a wonderful spread that you'll want to lavish on everything: tostadas, warm tortillas, crostini or crispy pitta – it even tastes great stirred through warm pasta. In the Yucatán it is called Sikil Pac, and it was demonstrated to us by David Sterling, a chef in Mérida, on one of our supplier visits there. This is our version, using ingredients that are available in the UK. It is amazingly nutritious and packed full of protein.

Heat a dry frying pan and toast the sesame seeds, stirring occasionally, until they turn a light golden colour – about 5–10 minutes. Some of them will pop! Transfer to a food processor. Toast the pumpkin seeds until light golden, another 5–10 minutes, then add to the processor. Put the garlic in the pan and toast on all sides until soft and starting to blacken, about 10 minutes. This will give your spread a lovely soft, roasted flavour.

Pulse the seeds together a few times until the mixture resembles coarse breadcrumbs. Add the skinned garlic, a good few pinches of sea salt and the chillies and pulse again to get a rough-textured mix. Pour in the olive oil, add the coriander leaves and pulse again. Taste and season with a little more salt if needed.

Use in this form as a dip, or you could thin it down with 500ml stock to make a delicious sauce for roast chicken.

Makes 1 small bowl
Time: 20 minutes

50g sesame seeds
200g pumpkin seeds
2 garlic cloves, unpeeled
sea salt
3 chiles de árbol or about 7 small Italian dried chillies or 1 heaped teaspoon chilli flakes
150ml olive oil
very large handful of coriander leaves, roughly chopped

Soft-baked feta

Mexico produces some serious cheeses, thanks to the efforts of thousands of farmers with their own small cattle herds. But rather than fly our favourite ones across the world to use at Wahaca, we like to seek out alternatives that are made closer to home. Feta is a great substitute for queso fresco in this classic little dish, and tastes outrageously good melted into the olive oil, absorbing all the flavours of garlic, lime zest and marjoram. Blissfully easy to pull together – and to mop up with some crusty bread or warm tortillas.

Preheat the oven to 180°C/350°F/gas 4.

Drain and slice the feta and lay it out in an earthenware bowl wide enough to hold the slices in a single layer. Finely chop the garlic and the herbs, and roughly chop the chillies. Sprinkle them over the feta with the lime juice and zest. Finally, pour over the extra virgin olive oil.

Bake for 10–15 minutes, until the cheese is soft and squidgy and smelling irresistible.

Feeds 4–6 as a light lunch, or more as a snack
Time: 20 minutes

500g good-quality feta cheese
2 garlic cloves
10 sprigs of fresh thyme
small handful of fresh marjoram or ½ teaspoon dried oregano
juice and zest of 1 lime
2 chiles de árbol or 2 teaspoons dried chilli flakes
120ml extra virgin olive oil

Pork scratchings

Chicharrón, aka pork scratchings, are the national snack in Mexico. We adore them too! If you love to eat and are not afraid of a little fat in your diet, then this recipe is designed for you. It's cheap too, as most butchers will give you the pork skin for nothing.

Bash the garlic cloves, then place in a saucepan with all the other ingredients. If necessary, cut the skin into a few pieces so that it fits more easily. Cover with water and bring to the boil, then simmer until the skin is completely tender on both sides, about 45–50 minutes. Drain well, pat the skin dry with kitchen paper and allow to cool. Scrape off any jelly or fat without tearing it. Now cut the pork skin into pieces (I favour small and bite-sized) and leave to dry overnight on a rack somewhere warm, such as an airing cupboard or above an oven

Preheat the oven to 210°C/410°F/gas 6. Place the skin pieces in a single layer in 2 baking tins and roast for about 10 minutes, ensuring they do not burn. Drain off any excess fat, turn the oven down to 160°C/320°F/gas 3 and roast for a further 20 minutes, taking care not to let the pieces get too dark and overcook. Drain off any excess fat, then allow the pieces to cool. This process is essential to get scratchings that really puff up.

Once they are completely cool, turn the oven back up to 180°C/350°F/gas 4 and, when up to temperature, cook for a further 5–10 minutes, removing the pieces as they puff up and brown (not all will, but they will still be delicious).

Eat with plenty of freshly made Guacamole (page 194) and a glass of good beer or English ale. The scratchings will last for at least a week in an airtight container, unless your willpower is like mine.

Makes 1 large bowlful
Time: 70–80 minutes +
**   overnight drying**

2 garlic cloves, unpeeled
800g pork skin, preferably
   from the hind leg, cut about
   2cm thick
1 heaped teaspoon black
   peppercorns
1 teaspoon allspice berries
1 teaspoon fennel seeds
small handful of thyme sprigs
2 heaped teaspoons sea salt
zest of 1 orange
4 tablespoons malt or cider
   vinegar

Stuffed chillies

These are spicy, hot and delicious. If you like, you can simply shallow-fry the chillies, but the batter is a Mexican tradition and really gives this dish the edge. Serve as a scrumptious nibble, or with a simple tomato sauce and a bowl of rice for a fun supper. In Mexico we ate them straight off the grill. Yum!

Make an incision near the top of each chilli, cut halfway around and then down to the tip. Remove the stem and seeds from inside, leaving the stalk. Put the chillies in a pan of cold water, season with several good pinches of sea salt and bring to the boil. Simmer for 5 minutes, until tender (open the kitchen windows – they give off a fierce vapour), then drain.

Mix together the 2 cheeses, the chervil and chives and season with a little salt. Stuff each chilli with a heaped teaspoon of this mixture.

Beat the egg whites until stiff. Add a good pinch of salt and slowly beat in the yolks, one at a time until fully incorporated.

Heat a 5cm depth of oil in a heavy-bottomed frying pan until hot. Dust the filled chillies in the flour, then dunk in the egg batter, spooning over any gaps with more batter until they are completely enveloped. Add the chillies to the hot oil as you batter them, a few at a time, and fry on all sides until golden (if they are browning too quickly turn the heat down). Drain on kitchen paper and sprinkle with a little salt.

Serve in warm tortillas with a mild salsa and some sour cream as snacks.

Feeds 4–6
Time: 30 minutes

12 large green chillies, preferably jalapeños
sea salt
150g cream cheese
30g Gran Padano cheese, grated
small bunch each of chervil and chives, finely chopped
3 eggs, separated
sunflower oil, for frying
1–2 tablespoons flour

To serve:
warm tortillas
mild salsa, such as Fresh salsa verde (page 224)
sour cream

Pickled vegetables

This punchy mix is the ideal light tapas to pick at with a drink before your food arrives, or add liberally to spice up tacos and quesadillas. Pickled vegetables appear to me to be very British (think piccalilli and pickled onions – not to mention our nationwide love affair with chutneys), despite being quintessentially Mexican. I am addicted to them. They are hardly any trouble to make and last at least a month in the fridge.

Heat the oil in a large pan and add the onions, cauliflower, carrots, garlic, chillies and radishes. Sauté over a medium heat for 5–10 minutes, until the vegetables start to soften but still have a bit of bite. Crush the coriander seeds, peppercorns and allspice with a pestle and mortar or in a spice grinder. Add them to the pan along with the rest of the ingredients, bring to a simmer and cook for a minute or so, then turn off the heat.

Check the seasoning, adding more sugar, salt or vinegar to balance the flavours. Allow to cool, then pack into a large sterilised jar (see page 174) and refrigerate. Try not to touch for 3 days as the vegetables mellow in their juices and become increasingly delicious.

Makes 1 x 1 litre Kilner jar
Time: 35 minutes + 3 days to mature

100ml olive oil
2 large red onions, halved and sliced into 5mm rounds
½ head of cauliflower, cut into small florets
2 large carrots, sliced diagonally
12 garlic cloves, sliced in half lengthways
10–12 jalapeño chillies, sliced diagonally
1 bunch of radishes, topped and cut in half
1 teaspoon coriander seeds
½ teaspoon peppercorns
6 allspice berries
3 bay leaves
4 sprigs of fresh thyme, plus a pinch of dried oregano (optional)
2 tablespoons brown sugar
2 tablespoons sea salt
1 teaspoon Dijon mustard
500ml cider vinegar
50ml sherry
250ml water

Guacamole

Mexicans use avocados in plenty of recipes, but guacamole is the undisputed superstar. In my experience, the secret to a good one is ripe avocados and masses of fresh coriander and fresh lime juice. Oh, and a pestle and mortar – the flavours need to be really ground together. With the essentials in place, this is one of those recipes that you can play around with according to taste: make it chunky or completely puréed – however you wish; in Mexico no two guacamoles are ever the same. I love our summer version with the fruity zing of tomatoes. At Wahaca we make it fresh, twice a day, as it doesn't keep well. It's hard to think of an easier, healthier, more addictive snack.

Check the heat of the chillies by nibbling the tip of one, the part furthest from the stem. If they are very hot, think about using less, or leaving out some of the seeds.

Put a quarter of the onion, the garlic (if using), half the chilli and salt in a mortar and mash to a rough paste.

Cut open the avocados, remove the stones and scoop the flesh into the mortar (or into a large bowl if your mortar is too small). Roughly mash with a fork, adding half the lime juice as you go. When you have a rough guacamole, stir in the rest of the lime juice, chillies and onion with the coriander and tomato.

Season with plenty of black pepper. If it doesn't taste delicious by this stage, you can add more salt, lime juice or coriander.

Serve with freshly made Totopos (page 50) or Pork scratchings (page 190).

NOTE: You can add many different types of fruit to guacamole. Experiment with those in season, such as ripe peaches, grapes or pomegranates.

Feeds 6
Time: 20 minutes

1–2 green chillies, finely chopped
½ red onion, very finely chopped
1 small garlic clove (optional)
1–2 teaspoons sea salt
3 ripe Hass avocados
juice of 1–2 limes
small handful of coriander, chopped
1 very ripe tomato, de-seeded and diced
freshly ground black pepper

Addictive, hot chilli nuts

These spicy, zingy nuts can be found in most cantinas in Mexico, and are salty and moreish enough to keep you drinking all night. We developed our recipe painstakingly, and the result is easy to cook but surprisingly impressive as a pre-dinner snack. If you prefer things less spicy, cut down on the amount of chilli. The nuts are easy, fabulously tasty and keep for at least a few weeks in an airtight container, so are perfect for patient party planners.

Preheat the oven to 150°C/300°F/gas 2.

Heat the oil in a large frying pan and add the nuts and garlic cloves. Fry them for 5 minutes, stirring with a wooden spoon so that the nuts are coated in oil and do not catch on the bottom of the pan. Add the chillies and fry for another 10–12 minutes on a medium heat until most of the chillies darken, then drain through a sieve.

Put the peanut mixture on a baking sheet with the thyme and salt and roast in the oven for 20–25 minutes, shaking occasionally.

Remove the nuts from the oven and squeeze over the lime juice. Leave them spread out to cool, checking for seasoning after about 5 minutes and adding more salt if needed.

Makes 500g
Time: 45 minutes

100ml sunflower oil
500g raw peanuts, unskinned
1 head of garlic, cloves
    separated but unpeeled
8 chiles de árbol, roughly torn,
    or a sprinkling of small dried
    red chillies
leaves from 5–6 sprigs of thyme
1 tablespoon extra fine sea salt
juice of 2 limes

Avocado and green apple salsa

I love stumbling upon surprising flavour matches, so I was pleased to discover this combination whilst working out a salsa for our herring tostadas. The crisp, fresh Granny Smith apple cuts beautifully through the creamy richness of the avocados. This guacamole is a stunning autumn dip or the perfect accompaniment to poached salmon or smoked fish.

Put three-quarters of the onion, chilli and apple into a mortar with a pinch of salt and gently pound to a rough but still slightly crunchy paste.

Add the avocado flesh to the mortar (or put into a large bowl if your mortar is too small). Roughly mash with a fork, then pound again, leaving a few chunky bits. Stir in the lemon juice and the rest of the onion, chilli and apple and finally the coriander. Taste and season.

Feeds 6
Time: 20 minutes

5 spring onions, finely chopped
1 green chilli, finely chopped
1 Granny Smith apple, chopped
  into small cubes
sea salt
2 ripe Hass avocados, roughly
  chopped or scooped out
juice of ½ a large lemon
1 tablespoon coriander,
  roughly chopped
freshly ground black pepper

Awesome avocados

Avocados got their name from the ancient Nahuatl word 'ahuácatl', meaning 'testicle', because of the shape of the fruit and the way that it hangs from the tree in pairs. The Aztecs believed that avocados were a 'fertility fruit', and warriors would eat them in copious quantities to boost virility. It turns out they had the right idea – avocados are so full of essential vitamins, minerals and good oils that their nutritonal value is indisputable, and their creaminess works as a wonderful contrast to spicy salsas and sauces. At work we love them so much that we often have them on toasted tortillas for breakfast, or whizzed into milkshakes (page 27).

It is vital that you eat avocados when they are ripe, so press the tip of the fruit gently when you are buying to check for a bit of give. If you can find only hard ones, put them somewhere warm in a paper bag with a few bananas or kiwi fruit to help them ripen. Before eating them, scoop out any black bits, as these don't look or taste very good. At Wahaca we favour the knobbly Hass avocados, which have a richer, creamier flesh than other varieties and are available at most good greengrocers and supermarkets.

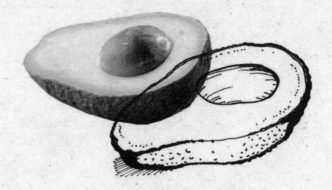

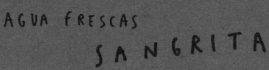

HIBISCUS MARGA

AGUA FRESCAS

SANGRITA

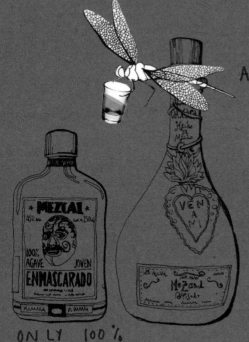

ONLY 100 %
BLUE AGAVE TEQUILA

In Mexico, drinks are a treat, not just because of the exotic fruits that can be used, but also because, when the sun goes down behind the hills, no better cocktails were designed to get a party started than those made from the heart of the agave.

drinks

This chapter is full of delicious cocktails that showcase the holy elixirs of Mexico: mezcal and tequila. For decades, these two spirits have been the most underrated of drinks. Cheap imitations flooded the global market, many made with a blend of different alcohols and artificial additives, acting like paint stripper on your teeth and a jagged saw on your head the morning after. Little wonder we were used to shooting them down with a wincing face and doses of salt and lime to mask their taste. Have a look overleaf for what these spirits are really about.

At Wahaca, we think making cocktails is just like cooking: you can experiment with ingredients, matching them to different-flavoured alcohols. Play around with these recipes and make them your own: try using different fruit purées and citrus to sweeten and sharpen the taste and different infusions in your tequila. At Wahaca we even like to experiment with sugars and use agave syrup for some cocktails for a mellower flavour; its low glycaemic index means it releases sugars slowly, and it has a lovely subtle sweetness. Little wonder it's one of Mexico's most successful exports.

The spirit of Mexico

Everyone thinks they know about tequila and a few about mezcal; many can't stomach the smell of either they have been so poisoned by cheap imitations. The good news is that the real thing, whether organic or not, certainly won't contain a worm, won't punish you the morning after, but almost certainly will have you leaping up and down for more!

Tequila is produced from the sap of the blue agave, a member of the lily family mainly found in the state of Jalisco, now a UNESCO world heritage site and tequila's main source. Mezcal (considered by many to be the 'mother' of tequila) is closely related to tequila but is made from about 12 different varieties of agave that grow mainly in the states of Oaxaca and Guerrero.

It takes about seven to ten years of basking and growing in the Mexican sun (and up to thirty-five years for some rare agaves) before the agave plant is ready to be harvested. Its large, spiky leaves are cut away, leaving the heart, or piña, which looks like an oversized pineapple. In the case of tequila, the piña is boiled or for mezcal, great pits are dug in the ground where the piñas roast for several days. The hearts are then mashed up and the resulting sugars that bleed out are fermented (in the case of mezcal) and either single distilled, or sometimes double distilled to make tequila or mezcal, a spirit so intoxicating that is has become one of my favourites.

Almost every village in Oaxaca has its own local mezcal, many using small-scale, traditional processes that are over 400 years old to blend the two ingredients: water and the agave heart. Some tequilas are also still made on small-scale production; we have some brands that claim that they could still produce their tequila with no electricity; the donkeys would keep pulling the huge stone wheels that mash up those agave hearts. Tequila often tastes smoother than mezcal as it is usually produced on a larger scale with more processes. The aged ones are laid down in oak barrels for an even silkier finish (see p.213). Some mezcals can be pretty fierce and smoky but the ones I love have a deep, warm, sweet finish to them; real mezcals should be at least 45% alcohol by volume.

At Wahaca we only serve tequila and mezcal made of 100% agave. The Azulito bar in the basement of our Wardour Street restaurant serves a collection of 80 of the world's finest brands, with examples of all ages and styles, from lowland to highland and blanco to extra añejo (see page 213). Whether drunk unaged, where the pure, grassy flavour of the agave is more prominent, or aged to produce a softer, more mellow flavour, the good stuff creates a rush of joy in the drinker that I can only describe as distilled sunshine. The most important thing to remember about either is that they should be sipped, not shot, to ensure maximum pleasure.

DON'T SHOOT

TEQUILA SHOULD BE SAVOURED
! BEWARE OF !
CHEAP IMITATIONS

full of ARTIFICIAL ADDITIVES

Just say no! IF YOU NEED TO ADD
LEMON & SALT
THEN YOU'RE DRINKING THE
WRONG TEQUILA!

Agua frescas

These 'fresh waters', created to slake one's thirst in the hot Mexican sunshine and rehydrate the body, are served at every cantina table in Mexico. Made from water, fruit, flowers or herbs and sugar, they are the most heavenly thirst quenchers.

Cucumber agua fresca

In Los Angeles, one of my favourite cantinas steeps cucumbers in water to serve as tap water over ice. It's a lovely idea. There is something intensely refreshing about the light flavour of cucumber, and this is a magical drink.

Whiz all the ingredients in a blender, then strain through a fine sieve lined with muslin. Pour into 3 tumblers and serve with plenty of ice and sprigs of mint.

Makes 3 glasses
Time: 5 minutes

4 English cucumbers or, better still, 8 short, fat Lebanese ones, which have much more flavour
½ serrano chilli or other green chilli, finely chopped
juice of 5 limes
4 tablespoons agave syrup
1 litre water
handful of mint leaves, plus extra to garnish
pinch of salt

Hibiscus
agua fresca

Hibiscus flowers, known as 'Jamaica' in Mexico, are available from most Middle Eastern grocers or specialist Mexican suppliers. They make a delicious, ruby-coloured drink that has a flavour somewhere between Ribena and cranberry juice. It is seriously popular at Wahaca, and makes the perfect foundation for a great cocktail (see page 207).

Makes 1 large jugful
Time: 35 minutes

60g dried hibiscus flowers
300g caster sugar
2.5 litres tap water
juice of 3 limes
sparkling water (optional)

Put the hibiscus flowers, sugar and tap water into a large pan and bring to the boil. Simmer briskly for about 30 minutes to extract maximum flavour from the flowers. Strain through a sieve, reserving the flowers to decorate the glasses, or to use in salads with a little caster sugar and red wine vinegar added to them.

Add the lime juice to the cordial and taste. You may want to add a little more sugar. Cool and serve on ice, perhaps with a little sparkling water to lighten up the flavour.

Tamarind
agua fresca

This is my favourite of all the agua frescas because it is so refreshingly sour. If you can't get whole tamarind pods, use tamarind pulp or purée instead. In all cases, you will need quite a bit of sugar to sweeten to taste.

Peel the outer shell off the tamarind pods and put in a large saucepan with the sugar and water. Bring to the boil and simmer gently for 5 minutes before turning off the heat. Whiz the mixture with a stick blender to break up the tamarind a little, then leave to steep and cool.

Strain the mixture through a fine sieve and add the fresh lime juice. Serve with plenty of ice.

Makes 1 large jugful
Time: 10 minutes

6 tamarind pods
120g caster sugar
2 litres water
juice of 2 limes

Margaritas

Here are our favourite and best-selling margaritas. As with
all cocktails, make sure you shake the ingredients over
plenty of ice – you don't want the drink to be diluted. And
don't forget to attach the lid properly. Many a barman at
work has been caught out by a loose lid when trying to do
a Tom Cruise impression from *Cocktail*. The aim is to shake
vigorously until the contents of the shaker are combined
and ice-cold, not wreak havoc in your kitchen.

NOTE: All tequilas used should be 100% blue agave.

When making margaritas, the first question to ask is how
your guests like theirs: 'straight up' is usually served in a
martini glass with no ice; 'on the rocks' is normally in a
tumbler filled all the way up with ice; 'frozen' is blitzed with
crushed ice – not very Mexican but a winner on the beach.

If you like a salt rim, you can have fun playing around
with various herbs and spices. Try grinding salt with piquín
or árbol chillies for a spicy rim to a margarita, or with sal
de gusano (worm salt) if you are making a mezcal-based
cocktail. For those with a sweet tooth, sugar rims work well,
and sugar plus chilli is an inspired combination. To get the
perfect rim, dip the cocktail glass into a saucer of water
so that only the very edge is wet, then dip the glass into a
saucer of whatever salt/sugar mixture you are using.

Tommi's classic Margarita

In this version of the classic, we use agave syrup instead of triple sec to sweeten the cocktail. The result is pure, refreshing and, we would go so far as to say, not bad for the health: with vitamin C from the fresh lime and low GI sugars from the agave syrup!

Prepare 2 tumblers with salt rims (see page 207). Shake all the ingredients over ice and pour into the tumblers. Garnish each with a wedge of lime.

Makes 2 glasses
Time: 5 minutes

fine sea salt, for rims
70ml blanco tequila
50ml fresh lime juice
30ml agave syrup
2 lime wedges, to garnish

Hibiscus Margarita

If you are a fan of our Hibiscus agua fresca, I suspect you will like this. The tart, cranberry-like flavour works spectacularly well in cocktails. If you can't get hold of hibiscus flowers, use any puréed seasonal fruit instead.

Shake all the ingredients over ice and pour into 2 tumblers. Garnish each with a wedge of lime.

Makes 2 glasses
Time: 5 minutes

50ml Hibiscus agua fresca
   (page 204)
70ml blanco tequila
50ml fresh lime juice
10ml triple sec
2 lime wedges, to garnish

Tamarind Margarita

This is definitely my favourite of our margaritas as it is so delectably tart and refreshing. A must for those who prefer sour cocktails.

Prepare 2 tumblers with chilli salt rims if you wish (see page 207). Shake all the ingredients over ice and pour into the tumblers. Garnish each with a wedge of lime.

Makes 2 glasses
Time: 5 minutes

fine sea salt mixed with chilli
   powder, for rims (optional)
70ml tamarind purée
70ml tequila
30ml triple sec
2 lime wedges, to garnish

Chilli chocolate Margarita

For those with sweet teeth and a love of chocolate, this is a splendid after-dinner drink.

Break the chocolate into a small, non-stick saucepan, add the milk, cinnamon stick, chilli and agave syrup and stir over a low heat until the chocolate has melted. Strain through a fine sieve and leave to cool.

Put the tequila and chocolate milk into a cocktail shaker and shake over ice. Serve on the rocks or straight up in martini glasses. Garnish with a dusting of ground cinnamon and caster sugar.

Makes 2 glasses
Time: 10 minutes

100g dark chocolate (at least 70% cocoa solids)
175ml full-fat milk
1 cinnamon stick
1 chile de árbol or a pinch of chilli flakes
1 generous teaspoon agave syrup or honey or brown sugar
100ml añejo (aged) tequila

To garnish:
ground cinnamon
caster sugar

Mojito DF

A riff on the classic mojito, this combines a mouth-watering mix of apple juice, lime juice and mint. DF is slang for Mexico City, or Distrito Federal.

Muddle the sugar, most of the mint leaves and all the lime wedges in the bottom of 2 tall glasses with a pestle or the end of a rolling pin. When you have extracted all the juice from the lime, pour in the apple juice and tequila, fill with crushed ice and garnish with the reserved mint leaves.

Makes 2 glasses
Time: 5 minutes

20g demerara sugar
large handful of mint leaves
1 lime, cut into wedges
70ml apple juice
70ml tequila

Sangrita

Add 140ml blanco tequila to this mix and you have a Bloody Maria (see overleaf). Alternatively, show your friends how to enjoy drinks the real Mexican way by making up a jug of this non-alcoholic base and pouring it out before lunch or dinner with small glasses of tequila for a delicious aperitif. In Mexico, tequila and sangrita are traditionally served in separate shot glasses and sipped alongside each other. In this recipe I have left the ingredients with approximate measures so you can adjust the spiciness to your taste. Enjoy!

Prepare 2 tumblers with chilli rims if you wish (see page 207). Shake all the ingredients over ice and pour into 4 tumblers. Garnish each with a wedge of lime and a dusting of chilli powder.

Makes 4 glasses
Time: 5 minutes

chilli powder, for rims
(optional)
500ml good-quality tomato
juice
juice of 1 large orange
(about 100ml)
juice of 1–2 limes
25ml grenadine
1–2 teaspoons Tabasco sauce
1–2 tablespoons Worcestershire
sauce
1–2 teaspoons sea salt
freshly ground black pepper

To garnish:
4 lime wedges
chilli powder

Bloody Maria
(we love it!)

The bloody Mary is one of the UK's most popular cocktails, but the history of this great drink is much disputed, with more than one famous cocktail mixologist claiming the recipe as his own. But stop for a moment and consider that the bloody Maria may have been the true original. Let's look at the facts:

1. The main ingredient is the tomato – and tomatoes originate from Mexico. It was the Spanish explorer Hernando Cortés who brought the tomato to Europe from the Aztec city of Tenochtítlan, which is now Mexico City, back in the 16th century.

2. Mexicans have been sipping the tomato-based sangrita with their tequila since the early 1920s, at about the same time that the original bloody Mary was 'invented' in New York. We are suspicious. We think that a lone barman probably strayed south of the border, discovered the delights of Sangrita and took the recipe back with him to NYC, where he created the bloody Mary.

3. Mexico produces the tastiest food and drink in the world, so it would only be natural that they had invented a drink as good as the bloody Mary/Maria.

There you have it – conclusive evidence!

The main difference is that the bloody Maria uses tequila as its primary spirit (as opposed to vodka in the bloody Mary), giving the drink a greater depth of flavour and the distinctive taste of the agave plant breaking through. Also, the bloody Maria is often made with a Sangrita base, so the tomato is flavoured with fresh orange and lime juice, in addition to grenadine and masses of Tabasco, producing a refreshing, spicy, addictive little cocktail.

To make your own, simply add 140ml blanco tequila to the Sangrita recipe on page 210.

Know your tequila

Blanco (white) – An unaged, clear tequila. Makes an excellent aperitif, and in Mexico is sipped with sangrita (page 210), a spicy tomato juice mix that complements tequila magnificently.

Reposado (rested) – Aged in wood for 2–12 months, this is generally more mellow than a blanco, with notes of vanilla and honey. Like wine, reposado can be sipped with food, and is a good start for someone who is new to the spirit.

Añejo (aged) – Aged in oak for a minimum of a year, añejo tequila develops a range of flavours, including vanilla, crème caramel and 'oakiness', while also slowly acquiring richness and complexity. In the mould of a good brandy or malt whisky, añejo is perfect for sipping after dinner or in some softer-tasting cocktails.

Extra añejo (extra aged) – Released in limited quantities, extra añejo requires longer ageing, which involves a careful balancing act to ensure that the influence of the barrel complements the original character of the spirit and avoids overwhelming it.

The Wahaca mule

Our own version of the mule, which we much prefer.

Shake all the ingredients over ice and pour into 2 tumblers.
Garnish each with a wedge of lime and a mere dash of
bitters – just enough to stain the drink.

Makes 2 glasses
Time: 5 minutes

70ml blanco tequila
250ml ginger beer
40ml fresh lime juice
10ml vanilla syrup

To serve:
2 lime wedges
dash of Angostura bitters

TO MAKE A CITRUS TWIST
Take a sharp knife and cut off the ends of the fruit.
Now cut off the peel from one end to the other,
shaving as finely as possible to avoid the bitter
white pith. You want to end up with strips about
1cm wide. Curl the strips around your finger to
make loose corkscrew shapes and use them to
garnish cocktails.

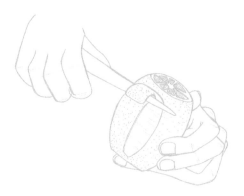

PEEL A THIN STRIP...

Smoked peach old-fashioned

This is a to-die-for version of one of the best cocktails ever invented. For those who like their cocktails old-fashioned, strong and with a hint of smoke.

Half-fill a large glass (or the glass of from a Boston shaker if you want to be pro) with crushed ice and water, adding a small pinch of salt. Put the glass inside the shaker, add the mezcal, bitters, gomme syrup and orange rind and top up with large ice cubes. Stir very well with a bar spoon for around 4 minutes.

Strain into 2 tumblers. Garnish each with an orange twist and serve with a small black straw.

Makes 2 glasses
Time: 10 minutes

small pinch of salt
100ml reposado mezcal
5ml peach bitters
20ml gomme syrup
rind of 2 oranges
2 orange twists, to serve
   (see Note opposite)

TWIST IT AROUND YOUR FINGER...

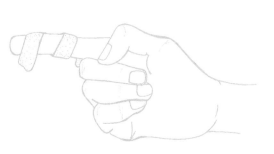

RELAX WITH A COCKTAIL AND ADMIRE YOUR HANDIWORK.

infusions

Here are four seasonal infusions designed by our old bartender Nate Sorby, and incorporated into his inspired spring, summer, autumn and winter cocktails.

Spring
Green tea tequila

We love Oolong tea for its rich flavour, but white tip tea is also delicious, and more delicate; jasmine tea produces something else altogether.

Put the tea leaves and tequila into a clean, airtight container and leave to infuse in the fridge for 48 hours. Sieve the tequila, discarding the tea leaves, then pour back into the original bottle. Proudly label and store in your drinks cupboard.

Makes 1 x 700ml bottle

**1 bottle (700ml) blanco tequila
60g green tea leaves, the best
   quality you can buy**

Green tea and rhubarb Collins

Pour the tequila, rhubarb syrup and apple juice into 2 tall glasses and stir well. Add enough ice to fill the glasses, then top up with soda water. Stir again and garnish with the apple slices.

NOTE: To make fresh rhubarb syrup, chop 500g rhubarb into small pieces and place in a saucepan with the zest of a lemon, the juice of half, and 5 tablespoons sugar. Cook over a medium heat for 10–15 minutes. You want the syrup to be quite sweet, so add a touch more sugar if needed. The leftover syrup will be delicious with Greek yoghurt.

Makes 2 glasses

**100 ml Green tea tequila
   (page 216)
50ml fresh rhubarb syrup
   (see Note)
50ml fresh apple juice
200ml soda water
green apple slices, to garnish**

Summer
Elderflower tequila

From about May, elderflowers can be found growing up and down the UK, even in cities, and everyone turns to making elderflower cordial. This recipe is much easier and produces the most wonderful-tasting tequila with which you can make seriously good cocktails and really impress your friends.

Put all the ingredients into a clean, airtight container and leave to infuse for at least 48 hours, or until the elderflower flavour has permeated the tequila. Sieve the tequila, discarding the flowers, then pour back into the original bottle. Proudly label and store in your drinks cupboard.

Makes 1 x 700ml bottle

**1 bottle (700ml) blanco tequila
50–100g fresh elderflowers**

Apple and elderflower fizz

Refreshing, floral and quintessentially Brit-Mex!

Muddle the apple with the sugar and lemon juice in 2 tumblers, using a pestle or the end of a rolling pin. Add the elderflower tequila and enough ice to fill the glasses. Top up with soda water, stir well and garnish with a slice of green apple and a lemon twist.

Makes 2 glasses

**2 small apples, diced, or
    50ml fresh apple purée
2 teaspoons white sugar
20ml fresh lemon juice
100ml Elderflower tequila (see
    above)
200ml soda water**

**To garnish:
green apple slices
2 lemon twists (see page 214)**

Autumn
Gingerbread tequila

I love ginger, so when Nate first created this recipe, I was overjoyed. The resulting tequila is fiery, smooth and sweet with notes of vanilla – totally irresistible.

Put all the ingredients into a clean, airtight container and leave to infuse for a week. When the flavours have permeated the tequila, sieve the liquor back into the original bottle. Proudly label and store in your drinks cupboard.

Makes 1 x 700ml bottle

1 x 700ml bottle añejo (aged) tequila
½–1 stick of cinnamon (depending on the size)
1 vanilla pod, split open lengthways
100g stem ginger

Gingerbread Margarita

For all those ginger nuts out there.

First make the ginger sugar. Mix the caster sugar and ground ginger in a shallow dish. Dip the rim of 2 tumblers in the mixture (see page 207) and set aside.

Put the syrup, tequila and apple juice in a cocktail shaker with cubed ice and shake well. Strain the mix into the prepared tumblers.

NOTE: To make fresh ginger and cinnamon syrup, put 200g sugar into a pan with 200ml water, a cinnamon stick and 8 slices of fresh ginger. Bring to the boil, then simmer and stir gently for 5 minutes, by which time the sugar will have dissolved. Set aside for 30 minutes, before straining and storing in a sterilised bottle (see page 174).

Makes 2 glasses

20ml fresh ginger and cinnamon syrup (see Note)
100ml Gingerbread tequila (see above)
70ml fresh apple juice

For the ginger sugar:
20g caster sugar
good pinch of ground ginger

Winter
Habañero and blood orange tequila

The combination of exquisitely sharp blood orange and fruity, fiery chilli is truly inspired. What's more, the Yucatán is a major producer of Seville oranges (introduced when the Spanish conquered Mexico), so this recipe is not a million miles away from what cool cocktail-makers might be serving in Mérida, the state capital, right now.

Put all the ingredients into a clean, airtight container and leave to infuse for a week. When the flavours have permeated the tequila, sieve the liquor back into the original bottle. Proudly label and store in your drinks cupboard.

Makes 1 x 700ml bottle

1 bottle (700ml) blanco tequila
½ blood orange
½ habañero or Scotch bonnet chilli, de-seeded

Yucatán sour

Perfection in a glass for those who like life a little spicy.

Put all the ingredients into a cocktail shaker and dry-shake (no ice) for 15 seconds, until the egg white has made the mixture foam up. Fill with ice and shake gently for another 15 seconds. Strain into 2 tumblers filled with fresh ice, or into 2 chilled martini glasses and garnish with orange twists.

NOTE: You can make a simple sugar syrup by heating together equal quantities of sugar and water and stirring to dissolve the sugar. Cool, then pour into a sterilised bottle (see page 174) and store in the fridge – it will always come in handy.

Makes 2 glasses

100ml Habañero and blood orange tequila (see above)
25ml fresh orange juice
25ml fresh lime juice
20ml sugar syrup (see Note) or agave syrup
1 egg white
2 orange twists (page 214)

CHILE DE ARBOL OIL

sals

Salsa is Spanish for 'sauce', but
that doesn't begin to describe the
thousands of recipes that are found
all over Mexico and that are so
fundamental to Mexican cooking.
Cantinas take pride in their house
salsas, which sit on every table
ready to ladle onto food. These
are either made fresh every day,
or special ones improve over time.
With over 200 different varieties of
chilli and 36 states all with different
influences and ingredients to play
with, there are seemingly infinite
numbers of unique salsa recipes
all over the country.

PINK PICKLED ONIONS

ROAST TOMATO
MOJO DE AJO

OIS

ADD A LIVELY KICK

Some food naturally goes with one particular salsa. The pork pibil that is so popular at Wahaca is always served with Pink pickled onions (page 231); carnitas are always served with salsa verde (page 224), and prawns seem a natural bedfellow for the slow-cooked Mojo de ajo with all its garlicky, smoky goodness (page 229). Beyond the tried classics you can get as inventive as you like, and a touch of salsa can dress up any dish, whether to add heat, texture or a light touch of freshness.

At Wahaca we make so many salsas that our new chefs become totally confused by which ones to put on what dish. Our red salsa is a blend of roast onion, garlic, tomato and smoked jalapeño chillies. It's a smoky, fiery salsa that goes beautifully

with our steak tacos, not to mention the chicken quesadillas. Our Black bean and sweetcorn salsa (page 230) is light, zesty and full of flavour, adding sparkle to ceviches, and a wonderful garnish for pan-fried fish. As for our Fruity, fiery salsa (page 240), it complements almost anything; try it on crispy potato taquitos or a baked potato, drizzle it on a quesadilla or over refried beans, or use it as a marinade for barbecued chicken.

Think of salsas as the equivalent of the ketchup and mustard we dollop over bangers, the olive oil the Italians can't live without, or the soy sauce that appears on every restaurant table in China. This chapter has everything you need to dress up your street food the Mexican way…

DISASTER STRIKES!

QUITE A HANDFUL

"CHILLY OUTSI
CHILLI INSID

ASLEEP ON THE JOB

Grow your own chillies

wahaca

Mexican market eating

It is no surprise that at Wahaca we love chillies. But we don't just chop them up and pop them into our food to spice things up – we also love to grow our own. Since we opened our doors in 2007, we have given away over 4.5 million packets of chilli seeds to our customers. If you have a packet lying around (or would like to pop by the restaurant to get one), it couldn't be easier to grow your own.

Step 1 Grab a suitable container. A seed tray is nice and fancy, but you can use anything from an old bean tin to an upturned hat. We've used a plant pot.

Step 2 Fill the container with compost and try adding a few old coffee grounds to the mix – they make a great fertiliser. Water generously with a fine spray and leave to soak for 30 minutes.

Step 3 Push your chilli seeds into the compost so they are about 5mm deep, then firm the soil over them. Go on, use your hands.

Step 4 Now keep your seeds from getting cold. Hug your container tight or, better yet, cover with clingfilm, which will hold in the heat and keep up the humidity. Place in a warm room or an airing cupboard.

Step 5 The waiting game. Within a week or two, your chillies should start to pop their heads up. Once you see those first shoots, remove the clingfilm and transfer the container to a light spot to continue the growing. Keep the soil moist but not sodden – a small spray of water every few days should do the trick.

Happy growing!

To get started, pick up your free chilli seed packs at any of our restaurants. For more chilli growing tips and expert videos, head to **blog.wahaca.co.uk**

Special thanks to (clockwise from top-left) Alex Plim, Anna-Lucy Terry, Heather Rainbow, Michael Anton, Nick Owers, Alistair Van Ryne, Jose-Paolo Roldan, Rosie Martin and Laura Halvey for their chilli growing efforts pictured opposite. Outstanding work guys!

Fresh salsa verde

Salsa verde is possibly the mostly widely made salsa in Mexico. If you can find fresh tomatillos, make this! It is an impossibly fresh, citrusy salsa with a lovely kick of heat – and there's no cooking involved. Tomatillos (a relation of the cape gooseberry) can be difficult to buy in the UK, but they are easy to grow in greenhouses or polytunnels, so if you have some outside space, get planting. This is great with the Tinga de pollo (page 131), with slow-cooked meats or grilled fish.

Set aside the coriander leaves for another recipe, then roughly chop the stems and stalks. Whiz in a blender with a few teaspoons of water and the rest of the ingredients until you have a rough salsa. Taste and add more salt or more lime juice if you think it needs it. This salsa should be eaten the day it is made.

Makes 1 small bowl
Time: 5 minutes

bunch of fresh coriander
5–6 medium-sized rip tomatillos
1 small white onion, finely chopped
1 jalapeño chilli or 2 green Thai chillies, stemmed
several good pinches of sea salt
juice of 1 lime

A robust salsa verde

This is the recipe I use when I can't get hold of fresh tomatillos. It is a more robust, rounded salsa than the previous recipe, and without its delicate freshness, so I use a habañero chilli to brighten things up and really make them sparkle.

Put the onion, chillies and garlic in a saucepan and cover in boiling water. Simmer for 5 minutes. Drain of all but a few tablespoons of the cooking liquid and transfer to a blender with the tomatillos, lime juice, sugar and salt. Blitz to a pulp, then transfer to a bowl and leave to cool.

Finely chop the coriander stalks, saving the leaves for another recipe. Stir them into the salsa along with the spring onions. This salsa will keep for a few days if stored in the fridge.

Makes a few small bowls
Time: 10 minutes

1 medium onion, roughly
   chopped
1 habañero chilli, stemmed
   and de-seeded
2 green Thai chillies, stemmed
2 garlic cloves
1 x 790g tin tomatillos, drained
juice of 1 lime
pinch of caster sugar
pinch of sea salt
large bunch of coriander
2 spring onions, finely chopped

Gooseberry and avocado salsa

I invented this recipe when I was desperate for some salsa verde but had no hope of finding tomatillos. Gooseberries have quite a similar flavour, but, unlike tomatillos, you can buy them all year round – from good farm shops in the summer or frozen in the winter. We are growing bushes in our London garden so that we can pick our own.

Bring a pan of water to the boil and drop in the gooseberries, onion and chillies. Simmer for 5 minutes, then immediately drain through a sieve and refresh in cold, running water for a few minutes.

Put the coriander, lime juice, olive oil and sugar in a blender and whiz together. Season well with salt and just a touch of pepper. Add the cooled gooseberry mixture and whiz to a purée. Stir in the shallots and avocado and check for seasoning.

Makes 1 bowl
Time: 10–15 minutes

300g gooseberries
½ small white onion
2 fresh green chillies
large handful of coriander,
**   roughly chopped**
juice of ½ a lime
2 teaspoons olive oil
½ teaspoon caster sugar
sea salt and freshly ground
**   black pepper**
2 small shallots, finely chopped
1 ripe Hass avocado, cut into
**   small dice**

Green herb oil

In Mexico they use an aged cheese called queso añejo to season street-food dishes and salsas. We use an aged pecorino, which has an almost identical flavour. You can buy good pecorino from cheese shops, and even half-decent ones in some supermarkets now. The chervil is not essential in this recipe, but its delicate hints of anise do give the oil a real taste of Mexico.

Whiz all the ingredients in a blender, seasoning to taste.

This oil is best served fresh, but it will keep for several weeks in the fridge. Just pour a centimetre of olive oil over the top to keep out the air, and therefore the mould.

Makes 2 small bowls
Time: 2–3 minutes

2 heaped tablespoons freshly grated pecorino cheese
3 bunches of basil, roughly chopped
large bunch of chervil, roughly chopped (optional)
2 garlic cloves
250ml extra virgin olive oil
juice of ½ a lime
sea salt and freshly ground black pepper

Mojo de ajo

This is one of my favourite Mexican sauces, flavoured with garlic, and lots of it, cooked so gently that it becomes soft, sweet and irresistibly good. I use this sauce in a huge number of recipes. It makes a mouth-watering marinade for barbecued chicken, and is the perfect companion for prawns and spinach (pages 98 and 151) – so good that even the most avid spinach-hater might be won round with this food of the gods.

Finely chop the garlic, taking care not to reduce it to a pulp if using a machine. Place in a small, heavy-bottomed pan with the chile de árbol, chipotles, thyme leaves and oil. Season with the salt and heat gently until the oil starts simmering. Now turn the heat to its lowest setting so that bubbles barely break the surface, and cook for 30 minutes. (If you cook over too high a heat, the garlic will burn, leaving a bitter taste, rather than the sweet, caramelised one you are after, and the flavour of the oil will be lost.)

Set aside to cool, then store in a sterilised jar (see page 174) for up to 3 months.

Makes 2 small bowls
Time: 45 minutes

3 heads of garlic, separated
  into cloves
1 chile de árbol, broken in half
1 teaspoon Chipotles en adobo
  (page 238, optional), finely
  chopped
leaves from a few sprigs
  of thyme
200ml extra virgin olive oil
1 teaspoon sea salt

Black bean and sweetcorn salsa

The combination of meaty black beans, sweet, ripe corn and the refreshing bite of fresh chilli and lime juice is pretty special. You can ladle this onto almost anything you like – barbecued chicken, salads, sausages, jacket potatoes – to give your food an extra special Mexican twist.

First make the dressing. Using a pestle and mortar, bash the garlic, chilli, salt and cumin together until the garlic is completely crushed, then add the lime juice, oil and pepper. Set aside.

Simmer the corn for about 5 minutes in a small pan of boiling salted water until the kernels are tender. Shave them off with a knife and toss in the dressing whilst still warm. Add the drained beans and the rest of the ingredients, and season to taste.

Makes 2 small bowls
Time: 20 minutes

1 corn cob
100g cooked black beans, tinned or homemade (see page 148)
4 spring onions, finely sliced
3 plum tomatoes, peeled, de-seeded and roughly diced
small handful of coriander, roughly chopped
1½ jalapeño chillies, finely chopped

For the dressing:
1 garlic clove, crushed
½ jalapeño chilli, finely chopped
1–2 teaspoons sea salt
generous pinch of freshly ground cumin
juice of ½ a lime
2 tablespoons very good-quality extra virgin olive oil
generous pinch of freshly ground black pepper

Pink pickled onions

In the Yucatán, this relish is used to accompany Pork pibil (page 132), which is probably the most popular item on our menu at Wahaca. The red onions, which are marinated in fresh lime juice, fresh orange juice and habañero chilli, turn a brilliant neon pink colour, which the Yucatecans use to brilliant effect in many dishes. Try them on grilled chicken and with slow-cooked black beans.

Cover the onion slices with boiling water and soak for 10 seconds. Drain and transfer to a bowl, then add the lime and orange juices and chopped chilli ((leave out half the chilli if you are not great with very hot food).

Season well and, using your hands, scrunch up the chilli in the marinade. Cover and leave in the fridge to marinate for several hours. Now scrub your hands meticulously or you will suffer the ferocious heat of the habañero!

Scatter the relish with chopped coriander just before serving. It will keep for several days in the fridge.

Makes 2 small bowls
Time: 10 minutes + 2 hours marinating

2 red onions, thinly sliced
juice of 2 limes
juice of 1 orange
1 habañero or Scotch bonnet chilli, very finely chopped
sea salt and freshly ground black pepper
freshly chopped coriander, to serve

Fresh tomato salsa

This salsa is fresh, lightly fiery and incredibly versatile. Make it during the summer, when you can find the ripest tomatoes, and store them outside the fridge so as to retain their naturally fruitiness. Use your best extra virgin olive oil for its delicious flavour, or sunflower oil if you prefer a totally authentic taste.

Cut the tomatoes into quarters and scoop out the seeds (these will make the salsa watery, so keep them to make a tomato sauce). Dice the flesh and combine in a bowl with the coriander leaves, onion, chillies, oil, half the lime juice, the seasoning and sugar. Check the flavour and add more salt, pepper or lime juice if you think the salsa needs it. Leave to marinate for at least 20 minutes before serving.

This salsa is delicious with almost anything: try it with black beans, grilled steaks and chicken, or served with Totopos (page 50) before supper.

Makes 2 bowls
Time: 15 minutes + 20 minutes marinating

5–6 very ripe plum tomatoes
small handful of coriander leaves, roughly chopped
1 small red onion, very finely diced
2 jalapeño chillies, very finely chopped
1 tablespoon extra virgin olive oil or sunflower oil
juice of 1–2 limes
1 tablespoon sea salt and freshly ground black pepper
1 teaspoon soft brown or demerara sugar

Roast tomato salsa

This is an easy, quick and really simple table salsa, the likes of which grace every cantina table across Mexico. Once you have a feel for how to roast vegetables on a dry griddle, experiment with different chillies to discover your taste and how hot you dare to go. Above all, have some fun and try not to kill anyone with excessive heat!

Dry-roast the tomatoes, onion, chilli and garlic as on page 82. Transfer to a blender, remembering to slip the skin off the garlic, then whiz together. Pour into a bowl and stir in the coriander and lime juice. Salt to taste – you want enough to provide a balance between the sweetness of the tomatoes and the zing of the limes.

WHY NOT TRY? If you want a deliciously smoky salsa, leave out the green chilli and instead add a chipotle that has been soaked in boiling water for 15 minutes. Alternatively, add a heaped teaspoon of Chipotles en adobo (page 238).

Makes 2 small bowls
Time: 25 minutes

3 plum tomatoes
1 small onion, cut into wedges
1 large jalapeño, or green chilli
3 garlic cloves, unpeeled
handful of coriander, chopped
juice of ½ a lime
sea salt

Burn your food

Mexicans like to burn their food, or char it at least. Seriously! When you are roasting fresh chillies, tomatoes, garlic cloves, onions and seeds, you really need to scorch them to get the unmistakable Mexican flavour into your salsas and sauces. If the edges of those veggies aren't a little bit black and charred you just ain't doing it right. So use your oldest pan, which you don't mind getting a bit blackened, and the next time you're told off for burning your food (as all my chefs were when we first opened Wahaca), just say, 'No way! This is the Mexican way!'

How to dry-roast

Step 1 Place a heavy-bottomed frying pan over a high heat and add whole tomatoes, chillies and garlic cloves (with their skin on to protect the delicate flesh) and thick wedges or slices of peeled onion.

Step 2 Turn the ingredients whilst they are roasting so that they are charred all over. Tomatoes take about 15 minutes, onions and chillies about 10, garlic about 5–10 minutes.

Once the ingredients are charred, you can whiz them in a blender (removing garlic skin and chilli stalks first).

NOTE While it's possible to grill these items on foil-lined baking sheets, I have never found that way as good as the traditional method.

Chile de árbol oil

As we are mad about chillies, it is only logical that we are mad about chilli oil too. Flavoured oils are really easy to make and keep for ages. At home, I keep a bottle by my hob to swirl into my cooking when I want a dash of heat. It is great drizzled over pizzas, salads, layered potatoes, fish and lots more.

Put the olive oil in a saucepan with the thyme, oregano, bay leaves and garlic. Crumble in the chillies, discarding the stalks. Place over a medium heat until the oil starts to simmer, then simmer very gently so that only a few bubbles break on the surface. You want to warm the ingredients together rather than fry them. This will preserve the flavour of the olive oil and stop the chillies from burning. Season with plenty of salt.

Cook for about 15 minutes, by which time the chillies will be smelling fragrant and the garlic will be soft. Remove from the heat, allow the oil to cool down, then pour the whole mixture into an airtight jar or bottle.

Makes 1 small bottle
Time: 20 minutes

200ml extra virgin olive oil
leaves from a sprig of thyme
good pinch of dried oregano,
    preferably Mexican
3 bay leaves
1 garlic clove
6–7 chiles de árbol, or 12 small
    dried red chillies
sea salt

Chipotles en adobo

'En adobo' means 'in a marinade'. This one is a simple-to-make, smoky, fiery, slightly sweet purée that harnesses the intense flavours of dried chipotle chillies. It lasts for months and quickly becomes an indispensable ingredient in the kitchen, delicious in stews, pasta sauces, dressings and mayonnaises.

Put the chillies in a saucepan, cover with water and bring to the boil. Lower the heat and simmer for about 35 minutes, until the chillies are completely soft, then drain and rinse off any excess seeds.

Put the onion, garlic, herbs and spices into a blender with 200ml of the water and 6 of the chillies and purée to a smooth paste.

Heat the oil in a large, heavy-bottomed saucepan until it is smoking hot. Add the chilli paste and fry for about 3 minutes, stirring continuously with a spatula to prevent it catching and burning. Add the vinegars, tomato purée, sugar, salt and another 100ml water and cook for 5 more minutes before adding the rest of the chillies. Cook, whilst stirring, for a further 15 minutes, checking for seasoning and sweetness. I like my chipotles to be quite sweet.

When ready, you can blend the chipotles into a purée, which makes them easier to measure out for recipes. Pour into sterilised jars (see page 174), then seal and label. Store in the fridge once opened. These make great presents at Christmas.

Makes enough to fill several jam jars
Time: 1 hour

200g chipotle chillies (about 65), stalks snipped off with scissors
1 large, Spanish onion, roughly chopped
1 head of garlic, cloves separated and roughly chopped
3 tablespoons fresh oregano leaves or a few good pinches of dried oregano
1–2 tablespoons fresh thyme leaves
2 fresh bay leaves
1 teaspoon cumin seeds, crushed
300ml water
4 tablespoons olive oil
350ml good-quality white wine vinegar
50ml good-quality balsamic vinegar
3 tablespoons tomato purée
7 tablespoons demerara or palm sugar
2 tablespoons sea salt

Hot chilli salsa

I must stress that this salsa is *exceedingly* hot. However, it makes a beautiful counterpoint to slow-braised meat and can verge on the addicitive. Pass it around so that people can drizzle as much as they dare.

Heat a frying pan over a high heat. Add the chillies to the pan in 2 to 3 batches, toasting very briefly. If you toast them too much, they will burn and their flavour will turn bitter. You want just to turn their colour and release their flavour. Transfer to a saucepan and add just enough water to cover, then simmer for 5 minutes.

Meanwhile, toast the garlic cloves in the frying pan until blackened all over, about 5 minutes. Slip off their skin, then place in a blender with the chillies, half their cooking liquid, spices and sugar and whiz together, slowly adding the vinegar. Serve (in moderation) with anything you fancy.

Store the salsa in a sterilised jar (see page 174) in the fridge. It will keep for a few weeks.

Makes 2 small bowls
Time: 10 minutes

40g small chiles de árbol
4 garlic cloves, unpeeled
1 teaspoon dried oregano
1 teaspoon peppercorns
½ teaspoon cumin seeds
1–2 teaspoons sea salt
1 teaspoon demerara sugar
250ml cider vinegar, or a
  mixture of white wine vinegar
  and rice vinegar

Fruity, fiery salsa

This is the most delicious hot sauce from the Yucatán, home of the habañero chilli. Scotch bonnets are almost identical in appearance and flavour, being wonderfully fruity and fiercely hot. If you are not mad on heat, remove the seeds of the chillies before chopping and use less of the flesh (you can always add more later). We love this salsa with almost anything, and it is surprisingly good in burgers or spooned over Refried beans (page 148). It takes very little time to make, and all the ingredients can be found in your local supermarket.

Heat the oil in a pan and sweat the onion and carrots for 10 minutes before adding the garlic. Cook until the onion turns translucent, then add the water. Bring to the boil and simmer until the carrots are soft. Add the remaining ingredients and whiz in a blender until smooth.

Store in a sterilised jar (see page 174) in the fridge.

Makes enough to fill 2 jam jars
Time: 25 minutes

2 tablespoons vegetable or
 olive oil
1 small onion, chopped
3 medium carrots, diced into
 small pieces
2 garlic cloves, chopped
500ml water
2–3 habañero or Scotch bonnet
 chillies, stems removed
juice of 2 limes
2 tablespoons white wine
 vinegar or good-quality
 cider vinegar
1 tablespoon salt
½ teaspoon dried oregano,
 preferably Mexican

Garlic and adobo sauce

This sauce – another winner from one of our head chefs' cook-off days – makes a delicious marinade for ribs, chicken and shellfish. I have fried whole spider crabs marinated in the stuff and they were amazing. I've adapted it from the original sauce by our chef Renan.

Make a cross at the tip of each tomato with a knife and cover with boiling water for 20–30 seconds. Slip off the skins, squeezing any juice from them over the flesh. Put the tomatoes in a blender and whiz with the rest of the ingredients, save 2 tablespoons of the olive oil.

Heat a deep frying pan and when it is hot add the remaining oil. Pour in the sauce, watching out for it spluttering, turn the heat down a little and stir for about 10 minutes, until it has reduced a little and the garlic has cooked out.

Cool and store in a sterilised jar (see page 174) in the fridge for up to a month.

Makes enough to fill 2 jam jars
Time: 25 minutes

4 plum tomatoes
**100g Chipotles en adobo
  (page 238)**
6 garlic cloves
1 medium onion
**½ teaspoon cumin seeds,
  freshly ground**
**good pinch of oregano,
  preferably Mexican**
1 teaspoon sea salt
100ml olive oil

Suppliers

When we started Wahaca it was extremely difficult to find the necessary ingredients. Chipotles, tomatillos, Mexican oregano, even corn tortillas were all unheard of. I remember having countless meetings with TexMex food suppliers, trying to explain to them that I didn't need a chile con carne mix for the restaurant, or a frozen guacamole.

These days the Mexican food bug has spread and people are really up on Mexican ingredients. I now get tweets about where the best suppliers are up and down the country, and at Wahaca we are increasingly being contacted by new growers of tomatillos, epazote, poblanos and jalapeños – these are exciting times for Mexican food! I have come across many of the suppliers listed here only recently, but they are all doing a great job.

Brindisa, for a range of Spanish food, including beautiful fresh chorizo, as well as guindillas and choricero peppers, which can be used to replace ancho chillies in recipes, and sweet and spicy smoked paprika.
The Floral Hall, Stoney Street, London SE1 9AF
www.brindisa.co.uk

Bristol Sweet Mart offers a range of dried chillies, plus tortillas, Mexican chocolate, pickled jalapeños, refried beans and much more.
80 St Marks Road, Bristol BS5 6JH
www.sweetmart.co.uk

Casa Mexico, 'Purveyors of the finest products from Mexico', offers a rich variety of dried chillies (ancho, chipotle, árbol, pastillo, mulatto), plus black beans, tortillas, totopos, salsas and much more.
1 Winkley Street, London E2 6PY
www.casamexico.co.uk

Chilli Pepper Pete wins kudos for opening one of the UK's first chilli shops and starting the National Chilli Awards. The shop and website stock a range of award-winning sauces, dried chillies, pastes, blends and seeds.
73 Trafalgar Street, Brighton, Sussex BN1 4EB
www.chillipepperpete.com

The Cool Chile Company is London-based and has a stall at Borough Market, a shop and restaurant in west London and a tortilla machine in Park Royal. They make the only real corn tortillas that I've come across so far in the UK. They rock!
139–143 Westbourne Grove, London W11 2RS
www.coolchile.co.uk

Edible Ornamentals were the first British farm to do pick-your-own chillies and sell all kinds of chilli-related goodies, including their own range of hot sauces. Check out their award-winning produce online.
Cherwood Nursery, Chawston,
Beds MK44 3BL
www.edibleornamentals.co.uk

El Azteca is a company created by Mexicans for Mexicans. Its website is in Spanish, but if you are interested in any of the products, you can get the Google translation.
164 Victoria Village Shopping Centre,
Victoria Street, London SW1E 5LB
www.elaztecafood.co.uk

Fire Foods, a family business, broke the Guinness World Record in 2011 by growing the world's hottest-ever chilli. Called the Infinity chilli, it boasts a Scoville Scale rating of 1,176,182 – that's pretty darn hot (an ordinary red chilli rates around 500). Order the seeds to grow your own, or choose from a range of wickedly hot sauces.
7 Darley Dale Crescent, Grantham,
Lincs NG31 8EH
www.firefoods.co.uk

Frida's Food offers a great selection of ingredients, from all the herbs and chillies you need to hot sauces and homemade tortillas.
25 Devonshire Close, Cawston Grange,
Rugby, Warks CV22 7EE
www.fridasfood.co.uk

Lupe Pinto's Deli has outlets in Edinburgh and Glasgow, as well as an online shop featuring a range of imported Mexican sauces and groceries, herbs and spices.
311 Great Western Road, Glasgow G4 9HR
24 Leven Street, Edinburgh EH3 9LJ
www.lupepintos.com

MexGrocer is a great, one-stop shop for a dazzling range of chillies and all kinds of useful ingredients: masa harina, nopales (cactus leaves), tomatillos, pozole and plenty more.
Tollgate Farm, Tollgate Road, St Albans,
Herts AL4 0NY
www.mexgrocer.co.uk

mmm... stocks some lovely food produce, including Mexican chillies, masa harina and tamale dough. Shop online or at their market stall. They are also alive on Twitter, where we first found them!
12/13 Grainger Market Arcade, Newcastle upon Tyne NE1 5QF
www.mmm-food.co.uk

Otami, located in Clifton village, sells all kinds of cool stuff, from colourful wrestling masks to funky textiles, plus authentic Mexican ingredients. A small shop that is hard to miss – worth a visit for its dazzling interior, friendly staff and one-off products, not available online.
7 Clifton Arcade, Boyces Ave, Bristol BS8 4AA
www.otomi.co.uk

Peppers by Post chillies are grown by Michael and Joy Michaud in rural Dorset and are sold during the harvest season, from late July to early December. In 2011 the varieties they sold were all habañeros, ranging in heat level from Dorset Naga, one of the world's hottest chillies, to Apricot, which has almost no heat, but a delicious tropical aroma and flavour. Order a mixed bag and you could become an aficionado!
Sea Spring Farm, West Bexington,
Dorchester, Dorset DT2 9DD
www.peppersbypost.biz

South Devon Chilli Farm is an amazing resource of fresh chillies, dried chillies, chilli sauces, chilli chocolates and chilli jellies. Over 10,000 chilli plants grow here each year, so you shouldn't be stumped for inspiration!
Wigford Cross, Loddiswell, Kingsbridge, Devon TQ7 4DX
www.southdevonchillifarm.co.uk

The Spice Shop in London is worth a visit for its wide selection of Mexican chillies, both fresh and dried, but beware – its prices are out of this world!
1 Blenheim Crescent, London W11 2EE
www.thespiceshop.co.uk

Wally's Delicatessen in Wales stocks a selection of chillies, pickled jalapeños, cooking chorizo and cider vinegar.
42–44 Royal Arcade, Cardiff,
S. Glam CF10 2AE
www.wallysdeli.co.uk

World of Chillies offers you the chance to grow your own chillies from seed, as well as selling a variety of fresh and dried chillies to capture the imagination.
44 Windsor Road, Levenshulme, Manchester M19 2EB
www.worldofchillies.com

Index

Page numbers in *italic* refer to illustrations

Acknowledgements

Without Mexico, Wahaca wouldn't exist. Every time I go back to visit this magical country I discover new states and learn about their history; I find new ingredients (especially chillies) and the regions that are home to them; I eat in new, exciting restaurants manned by talented cooks proud of the incredible wealth of ingredients they have at their fingertips, the raw materials of their trade. Mexico is a place where chefs come to learn about the food, and stay. It is a country that is continuously inspiring, challenging and fascinating. I am constantly overwhelmed by the generosity and openness of the friends I make out there.

Without Mexico, this book wouldn't exist, but nor would it without Wahaca. This year Covent Garden, our first restaurant, is five years old and it has been probably the happiest time of my life. Thank you to everyone who has worked for us in this time, for sweating blood and tears with us and for believing in our mad plans. Our teams have been the rocks on whose broad shoulders Wahaca has grown; our chefs have made delicious food for thousands and thousands of people, our front of house teams have created buzzing, vibrant places to come and eat. I've never had so much fun.

Thanks to Katie, Janine, Jo, Oli and Mims; to Carolyn and Gavin for extraordinary patience and dedication; to Rosie, for making my life so much easier and better and to Cecilia, for making Mark so happy. Which finally brings me to Mark Selby, probably the best business partner in the world; even if we don't always see eye to eye, we always have fun working it out and what a ride we've had.

I owe a huge thanks to Hodder who have been beyond patient with the deadline for this book which stretched about as much as I did. Nicky and Sarah, you were both amazing, never losing sight of the end book or showing any doubt that I would finally finish it. For Zelda who yet again proved to be the best editor and to Emma Knight for being boundlessly enthusiastic about spreading the word.

To Emma Miller for being ever ready for recipe testing, food styling and fun and for taking things off my plate when I juggling with too much. For Lisa Harrison and Malou Burger for the most beautiful styling and photography, to Phil, Pete, Roly and everyone at Buro for once again surpassing themselves in the design – what a beautiful book!

To the cooks and chefs in Mexico through who I constantly learn: Roberto Solis, Alejandro Ruiz, Enrique Olvera, Jair Tello, Margarita Carrillo, Pia Quintana, Alicia Gironella, Carmen Titita, Abigail Mendoza and Diana Kennedy. To Jorge Toledo for introducing me to so many great Mexico City restaurants where I have learned still more.

Thank you to Sam Hart for sending me to Mexico in the first place and to Sam and Sophie, Jaspar, Damian and Paloma, Rawds and Alex Garcia Ponce who were the kindest and most supportive of friends during my time there and since.

To Manuel Diaz Cebrian and the Mexican Tourist Board for so much help on finding amazing places to visit in Mexico and to Daniel Dultzin for his boundless, infectious patriotism. To WOLF and SUB-Zero for providing me with the most incredible kitchen kit and to my genius father for designing the most beautiful kitchen that I work in every day. To my family in general for endless recipe testing, tasting and honest opinions on the results and to Antony Topping and Claudia Young at Greene & Heaton for putting up with me and looking after me so well. Most of all to my husband, Mark, whose unstinting enthusiasm, loyalty and belief buoys me through all things. And to Tatty for appearing out of the blue and giving me more pleasure than I could ever have possibly imagined.

+ FROM THE MARKETS +
- OF OAXACA -
(WA - HA - CA)

MIND
BLOWINGLY
TASTY STREET FOOD

PLENT
FI
IN THE S
THAN
M

ALL OUR FISH IS CERTIFIED BY THE
YOU GET THE TASTIEST FISH, F

A MENU FULL

VIBRA
FLAVOU
TO
DISCO

A VIBRANT
FLAVOURS TO DISCOVER

TH FRIENDS

POWER TO
THE PIBIL